Table of Contents

How To Find, Interview, and Select The Perfect Hypnotherapist

By

Dr. David F. Newman, D. Sc.
Certified Clinical Medical Hypnotherapist

Copyright Information

Disclaimer: The material in this publication is provided for informational purposes only. Laws, regulations and procedures constantly changing, and the examples and suggestions given are intended to be general guidelines only. This book is sold with the understanding that neither the author or the publisher are rendering medical advice though this publication.

To SOL, WTP, TB, TS, EAS, JES, and Mila

If ever there is a tomorrow when we're not together ... there is something you must always remember. You are braver than you believe, stronger than you seem, and smarter than you think.

Thanks for just being you!

Forward

David Newman is a unique individual. We all are unique in our own ways, David is a special case. He is passionate about the practice of hypnotherapy and the professional training required to be a practitioner. At the heart of his practice is his concern that his patients get the best possible experience tailored to their individual needs and desires. To that end, he has written this book in plain English – a straightforward guide to choosing the right practitioner for you. He blends practical advice with humor and kindness.

To my knowledge, very few publications, perhaps none, address the vital issues explored in his book. For the layperson, hypnosis has much popular mythology surrounding its practice. David shows us the day-to-day world of hypnosis and hypnotherapy in a way which emphasizes its great potential as a healing modality and debunks many of the questionable assumptions about hypnosis in the popular mind and press. If you treat David's book as the consumer manual on the profession you will not be disappointed. This book provides a noteworthy and arguably vital service to the many individuals seeking the benefits of hypnotherapy.

James Burk
Washington, DC

Words Shape The World

The subconscious is a computer

Dr. John G. Kappas, Ph.D., and certified hypnotherapist, discovered that the subconscious is identical to a modern computer; the subconscious mind, however, has absolutely no limits for the degree of success or failure. Everything we experience in life is a direct result of the programming that has been placed into our subconscious mind. Therefore, if we don't like the program that a computer is running, we simply change the program. If you aren't happy with your life, don't continue to pretend that you are a victim. It is vital for everyone to understand that we are active participants and as active participants we either consciously or unconsciously make choices that directly lead us to the situation we find ourselves in. Before we begin discussing how to find, interview, and select the perfect hypnotherapist, please allow me to explain what hypnosis and hypnotherapy is and what it is not. This explanation won't take long; however, it will be invaluable to you because you will now be able to assess the quality and training of a perspective hypnotherapist very quickly.

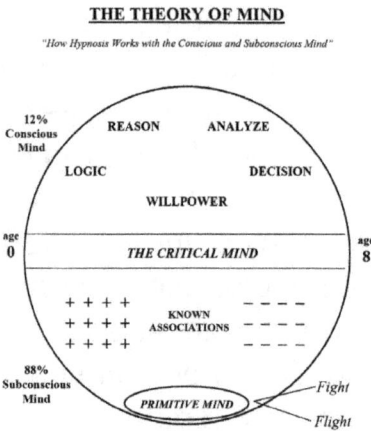

THE THEORY OF MIND

"How Hypnosis Works with the Conscious and Subconscious Mind"

12% Conscious Mind

REASON   ANALYZE

LOGIC   DECISION

WILLPOWER

age 0   THE CRITICAL MIND   age 8

+ + + +   KNOWN   - - - -
+ + + +   ASSOCIATIONS   - - - -
+ + + +   - - - -

88% Subconscious Mind

PRIMITIVE MIND   Fight

Flight

Understanding the conscious and subconscious mind

Looking at the diagram to the left, I would like you to pretend that the circle is a baby's brain at birth and that you are looking down on that brain. Looks kind of empty doesn't it? Well, the fact is, a baby's brain at birth is empty and both hemispheres of the brain are working in unison. At birth the brain is blank and the child does not have the mental ability to form critical thought. At this stage, the child's brain contains three items and all of them are specifically designed for self preservation. The first is located at the back of the brainstem; it only controls one area and that is the Fight and Flight response. The other two items that a baby is born with are phobias: a fear of loud noises and a fear of falling. Other than these three items, everything else is learned and if something is learned, then it can be unlearned and replaced with something new.

Critical thought begins to manifest

Between the ages of 7 and 9 years of age, the brain begins to form filters. I call these filters the critical cortex. Throughout our lifetime we will form thousands, if not hundreds of thousands, of these filters. However, let's focus on this first one. For those of us who have raised children, we recognize the fact that before about age 7 an authority figure (mom, dad, older brother or sister, aunts, uncles, and others) can tell the child the wildest and craziest story which the child, at this point, will accept as fact. However, when the child is somewhere between the ages of 7 and 9, parents begin to hear the magic and sometimes maddening word "WHY?" The child is not questioning authority but is forming the ability to have critical thought. The child is learning from all experiences and, most importantly, is beginning to develop the ability to project outcomes based on previous experience. This process will continue to be refined until at some point the individual dies.

The critical cortex also divides the mind and establishes a conscious mind, which is 12%, and the subconscious mind which, is 88% of the mind.

IMPORTANT: The subconscious mind controls everything in your body that you do not consciously think about. This includes but is not limited to: breathing, hormone levels, immune system, digestive system, heart rate, pain, stress, depression, thought processes, cell regeneration, blood sugar, and hundreds of thousands of functions that I haven't listed here.

How the conscious and subconscious mind work together
The conscious mind is very limited in its ability to capture information, process that information, and then record that information. This is specifically where the subconscious mind comes into play. The conscious mind is only able to focus on one task at a time. I know, "What about multitasking? I can do several things at once, like listening to music and texting on my phone or computer." Well, in reality you aren't doing all of those things at once. The conscious mind does not have that ability, however; it does change focus very quickly. Let me give you an example. Imagine that I take 6 ping pong balls and toss them all into the air at the same time. As the ping pong balls fall to the table they are not bouncing on the table at the same exact moment. In reality, they are bouncing

at different rates. This is what is happening when humans multi-task. Our conscious mind is bouncing back and forth between tasks very quickly, however; we are missing certain pieces of information. This is why when a student is day-dreaming, they do not recall everything that a teacher instructs them to do. The information did come in though the ears, but it was ignored by the conscious mind. The "missed information" is stored in the critical cortex. It is there, but the critical cortex is like a huge file cabinet, full of files and none of the files are labeled. The information is there but we really don't know where to look, so our perception is that we never received the information. Forty-five minutes before we go to bed at night our mind becomes highly suggestible and when we go to bed our critical cortex begins the download process to the subconscious mind. Sometimes we are aware of this download process, since clients have told me that they have trouble sleeping because all of the day's events are running though their minds.

The three stages of sleep and dreaming
The first stage of sleep is called twilight sleep. This is when we are just dozing off, yet we are still aware of some of the things going on around us. We are aware, for example, of people talking or the television going, yet we aren't really paying attention. Twilight is when the critical cortex begins to download the events into the subconscious. At this point the subconscious is simply receiving information and deciding if it will accept the information or reject the information. Acceptance of information is based on previous information that the subconscious has accepted as fact. If the information is congruent with the previous information then the subconscious

will accept the new information; however, if the new information is not congruent with previously accepted information, then that information will be vented out.

The second stage of sleep is called the precognitive state. In this stage, the subconscious has accepted the new information and then begins trying to predict future events and outcomes based on the combination of the new accepted information with the old information. Sometimes, the precognitive predications made at this stage are extremely accurate but most of the time the accuracy is sort of hit or miss. At this point all of the new information that has been accepted is called a known.

The third and final stage of sleep is called the venting state. In  this stage, the subconscious vents out the rejected information in early morning dreams. The early morning dreams are usually the ones we remember because we usually wake up either in the middle of a dream or just as it ends. These dreams rarely make sense and far too many people buy dream books and try to make sense of these dreams. In my opinion this is silly because all venting dreams are nothing more than the subconscious taking out the garbage. I do believe that predictive dreams can provide valuable insight into the subconscious processes and it is wise to write down these dreams if one can recall them. Allow me to offer a personal note. If I have an issue or problem and the solution has eluded me, I will focus on this for 45 minutes prior to going to bed and allow my subconscious to work on the problem all night. The results have been astounding and most of the time the solution suddenly comes to me the next morning.

Now you understand more than most psychotherapists, psychiatrists, family therapists, or medical doctors. So let me give you a few minutes just to enjoy your new-found knowledge and the power that knowledge contains.

Ah you're back. Okay, now let's discuss how hypnosis and hypnotherapy works. Here is the definition of hypnosis. "Hypnosis is an overload of message units that trigger the fight/flight response rendering the body into a catalepsy (the body seeming to be asleep and non-responsive). At this point the client (subject) is hyperaware of everything, but their conscious mind and all of the critical cortex filters have been rendered useless, allowing the hypnotist or hypnotherapist to speak to and to work directly with the subconscious mind. We call this state "hypnosis". While in this state, the negative knowns are vented out by the hypnotist or hypnotherapist and replaced by a new positive known. When this happens the results are both immediate and permanent." This is why it is so important that you find the very best hypnotist or hypnotherapist you can. Great positive things can develop when the person you work with is highly trained; unfortunately, negative results can happen if the person is poorly trained or has never had actual formal training. Here is a short list of negative results that may transpire by using a poorly trained hypnotist or hypnotherapist.

- False memories
- Transference of one issue or addiction to another
- Causing emotional pain (for example regressing an individual back to a very painful event and having them relive that event without establishing proper physical and psychological protection before the regression).
- Issues not resolved
- Transference of issues (for example, stop smoking and start drinking alcohol)
- Failure of the hypnotist or hypnotherapist to correctly identify when a referring issue is outside of their scope of practice and to refer the client to a health care professional for a second opinion and/or a medical referral (for example, when any of my clients are cancer patients, I always work directly with their oncologist on my plan of treatment for them and I always discuss in advance any additional therapy that I plan on doing and secure the oncologist's approval before starting that additional therapy.)

Who does hypnosis

The Traveling hypnotist
Hypnotherapy and clinical hypnosis has nothing to do with stage hypnosis that one sees at comedy clubs, high school graduations, or from the traveling hypnotist that moves from town to town, usually with their stop smoking and weight-loss sessions. I am not saying that these people are frauds, but their ability only works on 23% of the worlds population. For the rest of us, going to them is a waste of money.

Now that I mention the traveling hypnotist allow me to pull back the curtain and let you see them for what they really are. The traveling hypnotist is:

• Only trained to put one type of person into hypnosis: the Somnambulist. A somnambulist is a person who goes in and out of hypnosis very easily and often is very active in their sleep, such as sleepwalking. The somnambulist makes up 23% of the world's population.
• The traveling hypnotist travels from town to town putting on various "therapeutic programs" such as stop smoking, or weight loss. These programs are usually only one or two nights long.
• The traveling hypnotist charges very little money for their programs; it is usually between $49.00 and $60.00 per program. Most people will take both programs. Each program is approximately 60 minutes long.
• Each group session consists of 100 people.

- The traveling hypnotist offers a guarantee of their work: Should the session not be successful, you will be able to attend the next session for free; however, the next session is usually 400 miles or more away.
- The traveling hypnotist travels in a circuit and will return to your home town between 6 months and 1 year later.
- The traveling hypnotist earns in the neighborhood of $4,900 and $6,000 per program per night, and this translates to a total of between $9,000 $12,000 per town. Not bad pay for two hours of work.

The Stage Hypnotist
The stage hypnotist is a performer, an entertainer who uses members of the audience as part of their act. The stage hypnotist will do their best to make hypnosis appear as mysterious as possible and to promote the idea that they have "superhuman power" or control over a person. Hollywood movies have encouraged this line of thought and the stage hypnotist promotes this notion at every opportunity. Remember both the traveling hypnotists and the stage hypnotists work only with the somnambulist. Stage hypnotists are fantastic entertainers but I would question their ability as therapists.

Psychologists, Social Workers and Counselors
These three professions have received very specific training in certain areas. Let's look at each one for a moment.

Psychologists are individuals who have training in psychology. Throughout their studies they focus on theory, history of psychology, and they learn cognitive behavior therapy while they are in graduate school. All of their work is in what is known as "talk therapy", which is based on Sigmund Freud's theory of talk therapy now called psychotherapy. Freud was a hypnotherapist who felt uncomfortable that the client was in total control. He felt that the therapist should be more in control and guide the therapy. As one of the founders of psychological research he established psychoanalysis (which is falling out of favor with everyone except psychiatrists). Basically, all talk therapy is based on the assumption that repressed memories manifest themselves in undesirable actions or symptoms. Talk therapy works 38% of the time but only after an average of 600 sessions. Unfortunately, all therapists, with the exception of hypnotherapists who are not psychologists, CSW, LPC, MTF, or psychiatrists, are only taught talk therapy in a variety of different forms (CBT - cognitive behavior therapy, psychotherapy, psychodrama, and the list goes on).

Social workers have some training in psychology but they are more focused on the improvement of the quality of life and wellbeing of an individual, group, or community by intervening though research, policy, community organizing, direct practice, and teaching on behalf of those afflicted with poverty or any real or perceived social injustices and violations of their human rights. Most clinical social workers are licensed as mental health professionals.

Licensed professional counselor
The LPC is a mental health professional who has a masters degree or a doctorate degree in counseling or a related field. They must pass a state licensing exam and have the following:

- Academic course work in each of the following areas: normal human growth and development; abnormal human behavior; appraisal or assessment techniques; counseling theories; counseling methods or techniques (individual and group); research; lifestyle and career development; social, cultural and family issues; and professional orientation.
- As part of the graduate program, a supervised practicum experience that is primarily counseling in nature. The practicum should be at least 300 clock-hours with at least 100 clock-hours of direct client contact.

Doctors of Education
Doctors of Education are trained to conduct research in the field of education and often work in the public or private sector. Unfortunately, many of these individuals are now practicing hypnosis which, in my
opinion, is way outside of their scope of practice; however, armed with minimal training at best these people are now placing students (as young as elementary school) into hypnosis in an effort to correct behavior issues, and "make them better students." We have seen the disastrous results of these well intentioned but untrained individuals, attempting to correct specific issues without knowing how to do so.

Hypnosis is completely safe and it is a natural state that we all go into and out of several times every day; however, hypnotherapy (therapy while in hypnosis) should only be performed by a highly trained professional.

I am sure, you noticed that none of these licensed professionals have any training in hypnosis or hypnotherapy, but almost all state laws allow any mental health professional to use any method in treatment. This is one of the reasons why many mental health professionals will say that hypnosis doesn't work. Hypnosis works, provided the professional is trained in how to induce a hypnotic condition and then knows what to do with the client once they are in hypnosis. Unfortunately, most do not. Few have graduated from an accredited school of hypnotherapy, carries personal liability insurance, has proper business formation, or works as an adjunct to other members of the medical community.

Finding the Hypnotist or Hypnotherapist

The basics

In my opinion all hypnotists and hypnotherapists should have graduated from an accredited school of hypnotherapy. When I say accredited I mean the school should have one or more of the same accrediting agencies review and evaluate the program of study, instructor performance reports, testing, onsite library and in short be accredited in the exact same manner as any other school of higher learning. When this happens the quality of the student increases, the quality of the therapy is consistent, and results should also be consistent among all hypnotist and hypnotherapists.

Clinical internship

Participation in a clinical internship is vital for the hypnotist or hypnotherapist to become truly skilled in their profession. A clinical internship is additional hands-on training after graduation from the academic side of the program. At the school that I attended, we are required to participate in additional hands-on training in the form of clinical case studies. The clinical case studies allow actual individuals, who have a referring issue, to be treated by students while under the direct supervision of a Certified Hypnotherapist. More often than not the supervision is conducted by an instructor as well. This gives the student the opportunity to develop the skill, to accurately determine if the referring issue is really the issue or if it is a symptom of a deeper issue. The supervising Certified Hypnotherapist will make suggestions to the students plan of treatment, and quality of sessions. I hate to brag but I will. In my opinion the reason I am as good as I am, and as successful as I have been is directly attributed to the quality of instruction, being required to perform to established standards, and the clinical internship. The internship made all the difference and it taught me how to provide the best quality care for my clients. The minimum time that a hypnotist or hypnotherapist should spend in a clinical internship is 100 hours and if you can find a professional with more than 100 hours in a clinical internship program it is all the better.

Personal liability insurance
This is nothing more than malpractice insurance. It is required of every other licensed health care professional and I believe it should be required for all hypnotists and hypnotherapists. *IMPORTANT:* As of this writing I have been unable to find a single case where anyone has ever filed suit against a hypnotherapist's personal liability insurance; however, all hypnotherapist should carry it.

Typically a hypnotherapist should carry a minimum of 1 million and 5 million dollars. This is the same amount that physicians and other licensed medical professionals carry.

Why Personal Liability Insurance is Important
When a hypnotherapist applies for a personal liability insurance policy they must fully disclose to the insurance company the following:
• Verifiable education background including transcripts

- Speciality training for specific issues such as ADD/ADHD, Hypno-Child birthing, Hypno-Anesthesia, substance abuse
- Any previous complaints or litigation (past, present, or pending)
- List of all professional organizations and associations
- Office location
- Number of employees
- Specific treatments offered
- Number of years of experience
- Number of hours per week that the hypnotherapist works with clients under hypnosis
- Financial disclosures

The insurance company investigates and evaluates each application prior to issuing the policy. While, this system isn't perfect it demonstrates the level of professionalism that a hypnotist or hypnotherapist has. It also shows the client that some disinterested 3rd party has checked out and verified every statement that has been made on the application.

Certifications and what they really mean
One of the most confusing areas in the field of hypnosis and hypnotherapy is how freely certifications are tossed about. The reality is that certifications are primarily used in North America. The United Kingdom doesn't use them at all and neither do many other countries. In North America many professional associations self-certify. This means that if the hypnotist or hypnotherapist is a member of the association and they take a one or two hour seminar presented by a trainer of that association then they are given a certification for that specific issue.

Organizations that certify hypnotist and hypnotherapist
I have broken this list into two categories; Education (requires and verifies the professional's educational background and specific training in hypnosis and hypnotherapy. The second category is non-Education (they will certify individuals who join without performing a check on education or training. I would avoid hypnotist and hypnotherapist that belong to organizations on the second list.

Education Required and Verified for Membership

• The Association for Professional Hypnosis and Psychotherapy
• American Hypnosis Association (this organization does not certify the professional. They are only a professional organization specifically established for continued education of professional hypnotherapist)
• International Association of Counseling Hypnotherapists
• Professional Board of Hypnotherapy, Inc. (to join requires a minimum of 200 hours of education)
• Hypnotherapists Union (various locals) provides third party verification of professional training, and requires instructors written recommendation for certification.
• National Guild of Hypnotist (this is a self certifying organization. Individuals take classes by NGH instructors and are given immediate certification)

No Education Required for Membership

- International Society for Investigative and Forensic Hypnosis.Inc.
- International Association of Counseling Hypnotherapists
- Society of Psychological Hypnosis
- International Association of Counselors and Therapist
- Professional Board of Hypnotherapy
- American Association of Professional Hypnotherapists
- Association of Registered Clinical Hypnotherapists
- International Hypnosis Federations
- National Association of Transpersonal Hypnotherapist
- The International Medical and Dental Hypnotherapy Association
- Australian Society of Clinical Hypnotherapists
- British Society of Clinical Hypnosis
- National Board for Certified Clinical Hypnotherapists

If a person belongs to one or more of the Non Educational organizations it does not mean that they are not good or haven't gone though formal training; however, it does mean that as a prospective client you should ask more questions about their formal training, clinical internship, and how many clients per week they treat.

The Selection Process

What is a Hypnotist or Hypnotherapist?
Hypnotherapist and hypnotist have been specifically defined by the federal government in the Federal Dictionary of Occupational Titles. Published by the United States Department of Labor in 1977.

079.157.010 | Hypnotherapist
Alternate Title: Master Hypnotist | Alternate Title: Hypnotist.

"Hypnotherapist induces hypnotic state in client to increase motivation or to alter behavior patterns through hypnosis. Consults with client to determine the nature of problem. Prepares client to enter hypnotic states by explaining how hypnosis works and what client will experience. Test subjects to determine degrees of physical and emotional suggestibility. Induces hypnotic techniques of hypnosis based on interpretation of test results and an analysis of client's problem. May train client in self-hypnosis conditioning."

What is your suggestibility?
Suggestibility is a cornerstone of hypnosis and hypnotherapy. To be honest, if the professional doesn't know the suggestibility of the client, the successful outcome of the session is at best 50%. The hypnotist or hypnotherapist must know exactly how his or her client subconscious mind accepts suggestion. If the suggestion is not structured correctly the client's subconscious mind will vent out the suggestion immediately. Let me put this another way. If the subconscious mind does not

accept the suggestion from the hypnotist or hypnotherapist the session will not work and the result will be a total waste of time and money.

The four types of suggestibility are:

• Physical

• Emotional (also known as analytical)
• The Intellectual

• Somnambulist

Let me explain what some of the characteristics of each of these suggestibility types.

Before 1967, the world of hypnosis and hypnotherapy did not know or understand that there are three types of suggestibility; as a result professionals believed that only a small percentage of the population could be hypnotized. During this time, Ericksonian hypnosis was used which is based on deep relaxation combined with the hypnotist or hypnotherapist using guided imagery and metaphors in this specific form of hypnosis, to be effective the client must be able to visualize and use the imagination; however, not everyone has this ability. Emotional (Analytical) clients are able to visualize to a limited extent, but a subsection of this group, known as the Intellectual Emotional (Analytical), does not have this ability at all. I will offer a deeper explanation of each of the suggestibility types in just a few moments but first I would like to draw you attention to the diagram that was created by Dr. Kappas in

1967. This simple diagram literally changed the scope of hypnosis and hypnotherapy over night. Suddenly, the entire world is able to go into hypnosis, provided the hypnotist or hypnotherapist is properly trained.

Reviewing Dr. Kappas' suggestibility diagram we notice that the top line goes from 0 to 100 and represents the Physical Suggestibility of an individual. The bottom line also goes from 0 to 100 and represents the individuals Emotional (Analytical) Suggestibility. The line that goes from the 0 on the physical suggestibility line down to the 100 of the emotional (analytical) line represents and intellectual emotional (analytical). Very few people in the world are 100% of either suggestibility and the intellectual emotional (analytical) has a very difficult time interacting with

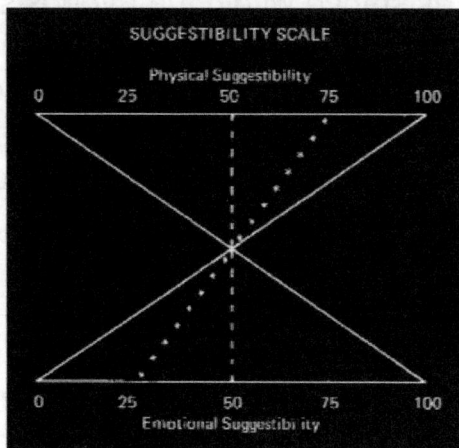

SUGGESTIBILITY SCALE

Physical Suggestibility

| 0 | 25 | 50 | 75 | 100 |

| 0 | 25 | 50 | 75 | 100 |

Emotional Suggestibility

people. The line that starts at 0 on the bottom and moves to 100 on the top line represents the high physical. The vertical line at the 50% represents the somnambulist. The somnambulists are 23% of the worlds population and go into and out of hypnosis very easily. It is the somnambulist that the stage hypnotist is looking for to bring on to the stage during their act.

This diagram suddenly illustrated that each and everyone of us is a combination of suggestibilities, to a greater or lesser degree in other words, we have a dominant suggestibility and the hypnotist or hypnotherapist must word each and every suggestion, induction, and post hypnotic suggestion based on the individual clients suggestibility or the subconscious will vent out the suggestion immediately and the hypnosis or hypnotherapy will not be effective. The exception to this rule is the somnambulist because they will accept either direct or inferred suggestions.

In 1967 when Dr. Kappas made his discovery there was much resistance within the hypnosis and hypnotherapy world. This shifted the responsibility for the success or failure of the therapy away from the "they cannot be hypnotized" to the question of the client receiving a secondary gain from the unwanted behavior, or the level of training of the hypnotist or hypnotherapist.

The Physical
The physical is a person who is right brain dominant and accepts direct suggestions. They respond well to physical touch and they need physical contact with others because that represents approval to them. People who have a physical dominance tend to express themselves bluntly and they are not too concerned with how others view them. When the physical dominate individual expresses his or herself they tend to be animated in movement and gestures and they move closer to the person they are speaking with. Typically they will dominate a conversation and barely listen to the other person. The physical dominate individual has difficulty understanding the emotions of others because, he or she can only relate to how they physically feel and not to what others say and feel.

Physicals accept direct suggestions

The Emotional (Analytical)
The emotional or analytical is left brain dominant and thinks things through. Typically the conversation that is going on in their head is more real to them than the conversations and actions of people in the mundane world. For example if an emotional (analytical) has an argument with someone, they will tend to replay that entire argument over in their mind carefully analyzing what they could have or should have said and what the response would have been. Once they have created every possible scenario and when they have found the scenario that provides them the best result they accept that result as reality even though it never really happened.

Emotional (Analytical) individuals uses their bodies as a defensive protection and unlike the physical they do not like to be touched and will physically back up if a person begins to move too closely to them during a conversation. Control is the operative word when dealing with the emotional (analytical) individual and everything must be logical, rational, and reasonable. The emotional (analytical) accepts inferred suggestions.

The Intellectual (a subset of the emotional (analytical)
The intellectual, for me, is the most interesting group to work with. As a group they are so analytical that they are almost unable to communicate with non analyticals because as they speak they are actually analyzing what they are saying as they are saying it. This demonstrates itself in day to day conversation as extremely long pauses between sentences and

words, long pauses when responding to what someone else has said in the conversation (by long pauses I mean up to 20 minutes long) and this group is almost void of facial expression. Of the world's population, 5% fall into this group. When this individual is in hypnosis they may ask, "Why?" after each suggestion. The reason is, even when in hypnosis, their mind is analyzing and the suggestion must be logical, reasonable, and congruent with their knowledge base. The intellectual only accepts inferred suggestions.

The Somnambulist
The somnambulist goes in and out of hypnosis very easily. The stage hypnotist uses somnambulists as part of their stage act because they do go into hypnosis so easily. The somnambulist falls right on the 50% mark of the diagram. They have neither right nor left brain dominance but use both hemispheres of the brain equally. The somnambulist will accept either direct or inferred suggestion.

Important: All suggestibility is learned between the ages of 0 and 8 and is rarely altered unless therapeutic intervention takes place.

Determining the suggestibility of a client
The hypnotist or hypnotherapist must first determine the clients suggestibility and this is accomplished though observation and asking specific questions. I have attached a copy of the suggestibility questionnaires that I use in my practice along with a scoring sheet in the back of this book for you to use. Physical and Emotional (Analytical) clients also present a pattern of issues. I have listed the most common ones that I

see in my office and the suggestibility of the individuals who seem to have those issues.

Physically Suggestible Subjects
Psychosomatic internal physical problems
Fear of flying
Fear of heights
Fear of closed places
Procrastination
Sales motivation Anxiety over exams
Rejections
Lack of confidence

Emotionally Suggestible Subjects
Psychosomatic external physical problems
Depression
Anxieties
Indecisiveness
Male and female sexual problems
Lack of confidence
Fear of contamination
Fear of death
Fear of loss of control
Obsessive-compulsive behavior

Working with the Emotional (analytical) suggestible people represents at least 60% of all those in therapy. Observation indicates that most conflicts are created by Emotional (analytical) suggestibility and even those who are predominantly Physical suggestible find that their emotional conflicts are cased by their Emotional (analytical) suggestibility.

The hypnotist or hypnotherapist must understand that if an issue has been caused by a person's Physical suggestibility then it must be removed using Physical suggestions and likewise if the issue is caused by the Emotional (analytical) suggestibility then it must be removed by using Emotional (analytical) suggestions. This is an area where most hypnotists and hypnotherapists, psychologists, psychiatrists, LPCs, PCs, MFTs, MDs, DOs, simply have not been trained.

Percentage of World Population by Suggestibility

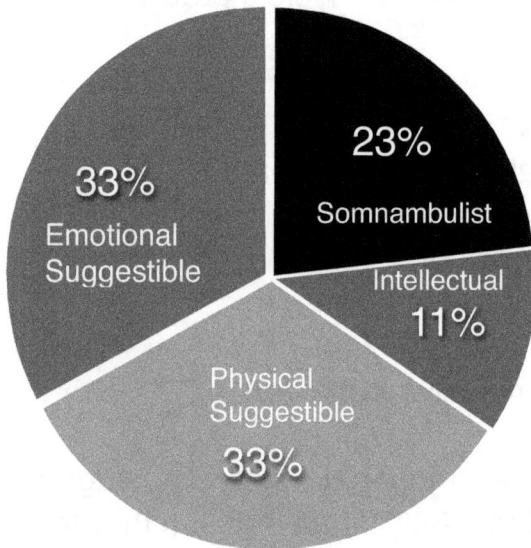

23% Somnambulist

Intellectual 11%

33% Emotional Suggestible

Physical Suggestible 33%

Finding your Hypnotist or Hypnotherapist

Beginning The Search

Searching for the perfect hypnotist or hypnotherapist is difficult. The difficulty isn't that
hypnotist and hypnotherapist
don't advertise but rather that
many mental health professionals, medical professionals, and
much of the general public think
that because they have taken a
few hours of training (even
internet classes) and received a
piece of paper saying that they are a "Certified Hypnotist" they
now believe that they are actually ready to work with people.

Let me ask a simple question. Would you go to a doctor who
just graduated medical school and allow them to diagnose
your symptoms, and prescribe a method of treatment without
them being supervised? Of course not. Medical Doctors
must complete 4 years of medical school a residency program
of 3 to 5 years before they are ever allowed to treat a patient
unsupervised.

Selecting a hypnotist or hypnotherapist, one needs to be just
as careful as one would be when selecting a medical doctor. I
would never recommend to a family member that they see

any hypnotist or hypnotherapist who does not have a minimum of 300 hours of study at an accredited school of hypnotherapy and I consider 300 hours the absolute minimum. All accredited schools can be found on the internet by going to http://ope.ed.gov/accreditation/search.aspx. In addition I think that all hypnotist and hypnotherapist should have a minimum of 100 hours of a clinical internship under the directed supervision of a hypnotherapist with several years of practice behind them.

Certification
Inquire as to the hypnotists or hypnotherapists certification. There is no standard certification process, nor is there any national or international board that certifies hypnotists or hypnotherapists. I recommend looking for a hypnotists or hypnotherapists that has certification by a disinterested third party such as the Hypnotherapists Union (AFL-CIO). The Hypnotherapists Union verifies the education the hypnotist or hypnotherapist has received, they demand proof of a clinical internship, and they secure letters of recommendation along with the hypnotist or hypnotherapist official transcripts which are sent directly to the Hypnotherapist Union from the school. After hypnotist or hypnotherapist has been investigated and everything has been verified the Hypnotherapists Union will grant a certificate as a Certified Union Hypnotist or Hypnotherapist.

Reviewing the website
Once upon a time, the first stop people made when looking for a hypnotist or hypnotherapist was the yellow pages. Now it is the world-wide web. So let's be honest, chances are that your

first stop will be the magic Google search for hypnosis or hypnotherapy in <insert the name of the city> ,and with one click of the enter key an entire list of people who all claim to be the most world renowned hypnotists or hypnotherapists will appear on your screen.

What does the website you are reviewing really tell you? Does it:

- Present a very professional appearance
- Is it presented in a clear, logical, easy to read manner
- Is the site specific and factual or it is vague
- Can you verify the information that is on the site though independent 3rd parties
- Is the professional's contact information easy to find including the address of the office
- Are there any claims of associations or certifying bodies on the site and if there are can you find their website so you can verify the qualifications
- Has the hypnotist or hypnotherapist written any articles that have been published and are they available on the internet
- Ask if this is all the hypnotist or hypnotherapist does or do they provide other treatment methods (you want someone who is a full time hypnotist or hypnotherapist and that is how they make their living)

Once you have done the research and verified the claims that the hypnotist or hypnotherapist has made it is time to phone the professional and inquire about an initial appointment.

Many hypnotists and hypnotherapists will give an initial appointment to you at no charge. Some do not. At RoseHeart Hypnotherapy Success Centers, Inc., in Jefferson City, Missouri we offer a 10 minute telephone or in office consultation where the prospective client can ask questions and get a feel of what to expect. We charge for our clinical intakes (first visit) and that is clearly explained up front.

What to expect from the first visit

The first visit is the most important visit for both the hypnotist or hypnotherapist and the prospective client. During this time the hypnotist or hypnotherapist should perform the following:

- Have the client fill out the client application and have the client write down specifically what the referring issue is; what they have done in the past to attempt to solve the referring issue, and what does the client want the hypnotist or hypnotherapist to do for them at this session
- The hypnotist or hypnotherapist should explain exactly what hypnosis and hypnotherapy is and isn't
- Determine the client's suggestibility
- Review a writing sample that the client provides
- Answer every question from the client
- Secure a medical referral if required
- Place the client into hypnosis and perform a progressed relaxation
- Draft a plan of treatment to resolve the clients issue
- Offer an estimate of how much the plan of treatment will cost
- Apply absolutely no pressure to book an additional appointment

Understanding what your subconscious is saying

The subconscious controls every aspect of your body and life that you do not consciously think about. When issues are repressed and not addressed the subconscious often will present those issues as symptom manifested in various parts of the body. The diagram to the left shows where these symptoms often present themselves. Personally, if I notice any body syndromes in either my clients or myself I immediately begin to ask what is it that I have not been addressing.

BODY SYNDROMES

The theory of *Body Syndromes* is based on the principle that whenever an emotional trauma is present, a corresponding physical reaction will take place. These physical reactions, called *body syndromes*, will in turn reflect the cause of the emotional trauma according to the area(s) of the body that becomes affected by pain, pressure, or tension.

Below are the 5 Body Syndromes. Please pick from a scale of 1 to 10 to rate each area and place that number along the side of the model.

| (10) the highest rating | (5) average rating | (1) the lowest rating |

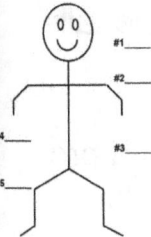

SYNDROME #1: "Crying"
Areas from the top of the head down to the solar plexus of the chest. This represents the inability to make decisions.

SYNDROME #2: "Responsibility"
Areas from the shoulders to the upper back. This often represents taking on too much responsibility or neglecting/not accepting it.

SYNDROME #3: "Frustration/Guilt"
Areas from the stomach, groin, hips to lower back. This represents sexual frustration or feelings of guilt for actions or behavior

SYNDROME #4: "Fight/Reaching"
Area of the arms, hands and fingers. This represents what you are holding on to, not letting go or pushing away in your life.

SYNDROME #5: "Flight/Running"
Area from the thighs to the feet and toes. This represents a need of wanting to escape or run away from a current situation.

Now you have visited and had a first session with a hypnotist or hypnotherapist one must ask themselves the following questions:

- Was my suggestibility tested and did it match my own suggestibility test
- Did the hypnotist or hypnotherapist really listen to what I said
- What type of hypnosis was used and do I feel that my session was productive
- Do I feel comfortable working with this hypnotist or hypnotherapist
- Was I presented with a plan of treatment that was logical and reasonable

- Was I told I had to come back a number of times for the hypnosis to work (if so run away from them fast)
- After 2 days or so do I feel that some improvement was made even though this was only an initial session
- Do I feel that I can trust this hypnotist or hypnotherapist
- Did the office look professional
- Did the hypnotist or hypnotherapist offer me alternative treatments such as massage therapy or Reiki (if so run away from them quickly)
- Was the hypnotist or hypnotherapist dressed professionally (like a doctor or lawyer)
- Was everything presented in a scientific setting
- Did the hypnotist or hypnotherapist present a calm and professional presence or did they seem focused on how long they have been working with hypnosis
- Did the hypnotist or hypnotherapist present me with a clients bill of rights (this covers expectations, insurance coverage, billing methods, and if they work with a sliding scale or not)
- Did the hypnotist or hypnotherapist clearly indicate that they are NOT a psychologist or medical doctor (unless of course they are so licensed)

How do I know if I was really in hypnosis
This is the most asked question I hear at my seminars, and when I guest lecture at universities, colleges, and in continuing education conferences.

"Hypnosis is an overload of message units triggering the flight/fight response that results in the client entering a catalepsy (A condition characterized by lack of response to external stimuli and by muscular rigidity, so that the limbs remain in whatever position they are placed). In reality the client is in a state of hyper-awareness and the senses are heightened to a point of almost super human level."

Nowhere in this definition did you find the word "relaxation". Relaxation is a result of the hypnosis but extreme relaxation does not allow the client to enter the hypnotic state.

Guided imagery is often confused with hypnosis which it is not. Guided imagery is used by therapists to help a patient remove themselves from the present situation such as the pain involved with Chemotherapy, or the stress of a situation such as a terminal event. In hypnosis and hypnotherapy we do use guided imagery but only after the client is in hypnosis. In this situation the hypnotist or hypnotherapist is specifically providing visual clues for the client as the therapy progresses. An example of this might be "imagine, or visualize, picture, or pretend that you are walking in a beautiful meadow. The sun is warm and you may feel the warmth on your face and shoulders. The meadow is full of tall emerald green grass that comes up to your knees and as you walk you notice the resistance of the grass as it wraps around your legs. You feel the resistance, yet it does not stop you as you easily walk though the meadow." In this example the client would already be into hypnosis and would be clearly visualizing this scene as clearly as if they were really in the meadow walking though the grass.

The level of hypnosis that the client has been placed into will determine how strong the visualization is. After one comes out of hypnosis one usually feels extremely relaxed and reports a strong feeling of well being.

The Interview

Not all Hypnotists and Hypnotherapists are created equal

Beginning the interview with a hypnotist or a hypnotherapist is very similar to the type of interview one might have when selecting a medical specialist like a cardiologist. Let's face it there are all sorts of medical doctors out in the world. Some are absolute miracle workers, some are super good, others are very good, but most are just average. Average is fine for most cases, but sometimes average just won't do. During the interview process the client will have the skill to know exactly the hypnotist or hypnotherapist level of expertise and more importantly which hypnotist or hypnotherapist you really want.

How to decide what level of hypnotist or hypnotherapist
The knee jerk reply would be the absolute best; however, if the referring issue is simply stress relief then depending on the training I would have no issue seeing a newly graduated hypnotherapist who is serving their clinical internship. If on the other hand the client has autoimmune disorders, cancer, pain management, or under medical care or prescription medications they will want to find a hypnotist or hypnotherapist who is the absolute best and you want to find someone who specializes in those specific issues.

Here are the most common issues that people have come in to see me about.

146 WAYS HYPNOTHERAPY MIGHT HELP YOU

1. Self-Confidence
2. Motivation
3. Self-Image
4. Stress
5. Anger
6. Frustration
7. Worry
8. Guilt
9. Forgiveness
10. Nail Biting
11. Anxiety
12. Assertiveness
13. Public Speaking
14. Memory
15. Concentration
16. Lower Blood Pressure
17. Smoking
18. Stage Fright
19. Reach Goals
20. Procrastination
21. Change Habits
22. Improve Sales
23. Attitude Adjustment
24. Career Success
25. Exam Anxiety
26. Relationship Enhancement
27. Hair Twisting
28. Nausea
29. Surgical Recovery
30. Tardiness
31. Gambling
32. Performance Anxiety
33. Perfectionism
34. Lack of Initiative

35. Self-Expression
36. Helplessness
37. Hopelessness
38. Overly Critical
39. Negativism
40. Death or Loss
41. Weight Loss
42. Substance Abuse
43. Study Habits
44. Fears
45. Phobias
46. Insomnia
47. Pain Management
48. Sports
49. Stuttering
50. Fear of Dentist
51. Fear of Doctor
52. Fear of Surgery
53. Assist Healing
54. Impotency
55. Child Birth
56. Sexual Problems
57. Agoraphobia
58. Obsessions
59. Passive-Aggressive
60. Obsessive-Compulsive
61. Relaxation
62. Addictions
63. Improve Health
64. Bed Wetting
65. Sleep Disorders

66. Skin Problems
67. Medication Side Effects
68. Premature Ejaculation
69. Inhibitions
70. Fear of Flying
71. Fear of Heights
72. Fear of Water
73. Fear of Animals
74. Communication
75. Self-Defeating Behaviors
76. Self-Criticism
77. Irritability
78. Pessimism
79. Controlling
80. Social Phobia
81. Panic Attacks
82. Temptation
83. Hypochondria
84. Self-Awareness
85. Aggression
86. Self-Esteem
87. Self-Blame
88. Hostility
89. Moodiness
90. Overeating
91. Age Regression
92. Past Life Regression
93. Irrational thoughts
94. Lack of Enthusiasm
95. Lack of Direction
96. Ulcers

127. Self-Hypnosis
128. Restlessness
129. Sadness
130. Insecurity
131. Mistrust
132. Victimization
133. Anesthesia
134. Biofeedback
135. Presurgical
136. Postsurgical
137. Cramps
138. Gagging
139. Dreams
140. Nightmares
141. Headaches
142. Immune System
143. Fear of Death
144. Relaxation
145. Breathing
146. Self-Mastery

If you wish to see a hypnotist or hypnotherapist for one of the 146 most common issues it's important that you explain to your hypnotist or hypnotherapist exactly what the issue is that you would like resolved. Be painfully honest with your therapist about when you noticed the issues, what you have done to resolve them, how well the solution you tried worked or didn't work. Basically, give the therapist as much information as you can, even if talking about it is painful. Trust me the results will be miraculous .

Sometimes, referring issues are really symptoms of deeper issues. For example, a client who comes in for smoking cessation may have several additional issues. A few possible issues where people self medicate by smoking are:

• Hypoglycemia (low blood sugar)
• Emotional or physical pain
• Worry
• Depression
• Sadness
• Lack of Joy

Are there additional issues not included on this list? Absolutely, but only a highly trained Hypnotherapist is qualified to evaluate. The reason the client has turned to tobacco is simple. The answer is sugar! Tobacco in North America is cured in sugar and 3% of every cigarette is pure sugar. Smokeless tobacco is even higher. The sugar enters the blood stream very quickly and immediately goes to the brain where the sugar stimulates the release of endorphins (endogenous opioid peptides that function as neurotransmitters and gives the individual the feeling of pleasure). The reason I mention this is that smoking is really self medication for one of the above actual issues. In this case smoking provides a secondary gain to the individual and it will be difficult to have them quit smoking until the actual issue or issues are resolved.

The final selection

Let the adventure begin

Developing your fullest potential

Hypnosis and hypnotherapy achieve results quickly, so the idea that you will be seeing a hypnotist or a hypnotherapist for years really is a misconception. As the chart shows, hypnosis and hypnotherapy are very effective in resolving issues quickly; however, it is even more effective in allowing the individual to live up to their highest potential.

Firing up the success factor

Everyone is 100% successful! Wow, what a claim. I know what you are thinking; how about the homeless living on the streets or in a shelter, how about the person in a dead end job, or how about the unemployed? There are literally thousands of examples of good people, qualified people, intelligent people who are living way below their potential. Yet I have the audacity to say they are 100% successful. Okay, let me explain.

Referring to the illustration below, we have two examples.
The dark line
and the lighter line are identical at birth and are mostly identical a person has their first job.

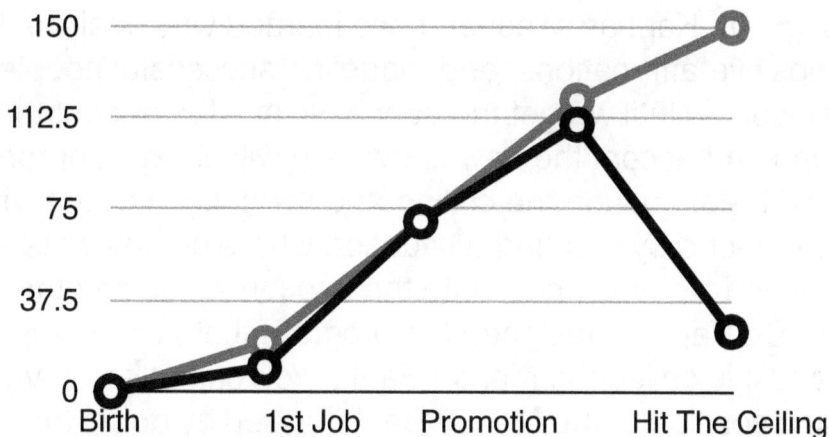

150				
112.5				
75				
37.5				
0	Birth	1st Job	Promotion	Hit The Ceiling

All of us have a floor, a point where the subconscious will not allow us to go below, and we have a ceiling-the highest point of success where the subconscious feels comfortable and will not take corrective action. Throughout our entire life we continue to rise and fall somewhere between the floor and the ceiling and we refer to this area as the comfort zone. This is where the subconscious feels very comfortable. When we approach the ceiling of our success the subconscious begins to create small acts of sabotage to bring us back down towards the middle zone where the subconscious feels most comfortable.

The hypnotherapist (not the hypnotist) is a subconscious behaviorist and is uniquely qualified to teach you the client how to continually raise your subconscious ceiling. As the subconscious ceiling is raised the subconscious never begins to sabotage because we never hit or breakthrough the ceiling. This allows the individual to continue to rise to their fullest potential.

Through Dr. Kappas's research we learned why positive thinking, positive affirmations, and modeling successful people rarely work. Until we get the subconscious to vent out the old knownd and accept the new known we will always approach, hit, and break though the ceiling and the subconscious will always respond by creating a situation where our success wanes and we move back into the subconscious comfort zone. Dr. Kappas designed the program that I use in my practice and it is called the Mental Bank. You can attend a video training session of the Mental Bank for free by going to http://www.mymentalbank.com This video is offered as a public service by the Hypnosis Motivation Institute, the first nationally accredited school of hypnotherapy in the United States. I encourage you to take the time to review this video and implement the lessons into your life. It only takes 3-5 minutes forty-five minutes before going to bed to make some unbelievable improvements in your life. If you do start the Mental Bank I want to give you this warning. Your subconscious is resistant to change and even though the Mental Bank only takes 3 minutes per night to complete, the subconscious will arrange ways to make you forget, make you too tired or anyone of a 1000 other ways to get you to stop. Just understand that this is normal and you have not failed; you just have to pick yourself up and begin again.

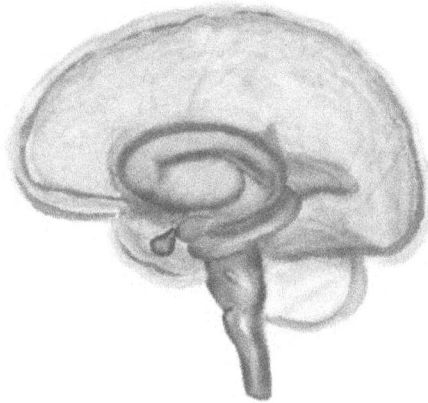

To
Change your Life...Change your Thoughts

What to expect

As you think so you are

I have one the best professions in the world. I work with athletes, actors, students, lawyers, police, parents, executives, sales people, and everyone in between. All of these people have one goal in common. They all want to maximize their potential while minimizing failures and setbacks. The best way for you to understand the power of your own subconscious mind is for me to give you actual examples of what can happen when you work with your Perfect Hypnotherapist. The changes you see will happen; however,the changes will be gentle, almost happening totally unnoticed by you until it suddenly hits you that you aren't doing what you used to do. You aren't eating the same foods or the same types of foods.

Power of the Subconscious

The illustration to the left illustrates every area that makes up the subconscious mind. The conscious mind, however, is located in the frontal lobe. The subconscious mind is responsible for everything that is not consciously thought of. Breathing, emotions, muscle coordination, flight or fight, survival response, hormones, immune system and the list just goes on. As I mentioned before, the subconscious mind makes up 88% plus or minus 3% of your mind. For true and total success in anything we have to get the subconscious on board and when that happens, truly amazing things manifest into reality.

How the Subconscious works

The subconscious works quietly. If you are expecting to see wild changes immediately then you will be disappointed. The subconscious works quietly. Once the subconscious has accepted the suggestions as knowns, you behavior changes. You may or may not be aware of the change until one day you simply realize that you are doing the new behavior and the realization hits you that Wow! I never used to do that. I have had clients who do not eat certain healthy foods, a week after our session, they report to me that for whatever reason they found themselves eating the healthy foods that before they never would have touched. Strangely, they enjoyed eating them. That is how the subconscious works. Quietly and efficiently. Let me give you an example with a sports team I have worked with.

The no show basketball team

Lincoln University is located in Jefferson City, Missouri. As universities go it really isn't ranked very high. Here is the history of the school:

At the close of the Civil War, soldiers and officers of the 62nd United States Colored Infantry, stationed at Fort McIntosh, Texas, but composed primarily of Missourians, took steps to establish an educational institution in Jefferson City, Missouri, which they named Lincoln Institute. The following stipulations were set for the school:
1. The institution shall be designed for the special benefit of the freed African-Americans;
2. It shall be located in the state of Missouri;
3. Its fundamental idea shall be to combine study and labor.

Members of the 62nd Colored Infantry contributed $5,000; this was supplemented by approximately $1,400, given by the 65th Colored Infantry.

On January 14, 1866, Lincoln Institute was formally established under an organization committee. By June of the same year, it incorporated and the committee became a Board of Trustees. Richard Baxter Foster, a former first lieutenant in the 62nd Infantry, was named first principal of Lincoln Institute. On September 17, 1866, the school opened its doors to the first class in an old frame building in Jefferson City.

In 1869, Lincoln Institute moved to the present campus, and in 1870 it began to receive aid from the state of Missouri for teacher training. College-level work was added to the curriculum in 1877, and passage of the Normal School Law permitted Lincoln graduates to teach for life in Missouri without further examination. Lincoln Institute formally became a state institution in 1879 with the deeding of the property to the state. Under the second Morrill Act of 1890, Lincoln became a land grant institution, and the following year industrial and agricultural courses were added to the curriculum.

In 1921, the Missouri Legislature passed a bill introduced by Walthall M. Moore, the first black American to serve in that body, which changed the name from Lincoln Institute to Lincoln University and created a Board of Curators to govern the University.

The North Central Association of Colleges and Secondary Schools accredited the high school division in 1925, the teacher-training program in 1926, and the four-year college of arts and sciences in 1934. Graduate instruction was begun in the summer session of 1940, with majors in education and history and minors in English, history, and sociology. A School of Journalism was established in February 1942.

In 1954, the United States Supreme Court handed down its ruling in Brown v. Board of Education, and Lincoln University responded by opening its doors to all applicably meeting its entrance criteria. Today, Lincoln University serves a diverse clientele, both residential and non-residential, engages in a variety of research projects, and offers numerous public service programs in addition to providing an array of academic programs.

While the history of the institution is rich and the students come from a highly diverse background most are international students or minorities from across the United States. Because Lincoln University isn't a top-ranked university the calibre of students varies greatly. The same is true with their athletic department. Most of the students that participate in the various athletic disciplines come from lower socially economic environments where education was not stressed. Most of these individuals are likable but they are starved for attention, combative, selfish, and are not team players at all. The result is a losing athletic department.

Okay I believe that I have described the referring issues well enough for you to appreciate the task at hand. I as part of RoseHeart Hypnotherapy Success Centers, community outreach, provided the athletic department with the opportunity to have a hypnotherapist work directly with their teams and individual athletes. The result was that the coach of the women's basketball team accepted the offer. During the initial interview she said that her team had potential but they refused to work as a team, and they simply didn't believe they could win. She further explained that the school administration and staff didn't even show up at the home games. The coach looked at me and said, "my girls could be winners but they don't believe they can be". I asked to meet the team that afternoon.

We started off with a group session before practice and the coach saw immediate improvement. Then I began working with each team member individually on their game but also on their study habits, test taking, and rewriting their life script for success. I met with the team an additional four times, and each individual team member two additional times. The results are astounding. For the first time in the history of the university their team won. They also won the state championship. The team worked as a team, each one a physical extension of the other. They dominated the court and would steal the ball in a nano second. Individually the girls elevated their academic standing by a minimum of two full grade points and for the first time in the history of the school these ladies won academic achievement awards and scholarships to graduate schools.

Thirteen young women met with me on that first day. Many of them were afraid of flunking out of school, none of them believed that their team could have a winning season, and the thought of taking the state championship was beyond their imagination. Yet, once these individuals subconscious minds accepted that they were winners, successful students, and very capable of achievement, we initiated the program for them to continue to raise their success ceiling. The sky was the limit. I should mention that after the team won the state championship their coach was immediately offered the head coaching position at Missouri State University at St. Louis which she accepted. So everyone's dreams came true.

Hypnotherapy for behavior modification

Smoking Cessation

I see lots of people who want to stop smoking. To my surprise most people think that is the only reason to see a hypnotist or a hypnotherapist. People smoke for a number of reasons; contrary to the marketing and what a number of professionals say addiction to nicotine is rarely the reason people don't seem to be able to stop smoking. Nicotine is a naturally occurring substance in our body. Each cell has nicotine receptors in them, but nicotine it isn't the reason for people feeling calmer once they take a drag off of their smoke. Nicotine is a stimulant when taken in small doses such as cigarettes. Nicotine when taken in larger doses nicotine overstimulate the body, triggering the fight or flight response and then nicotine acts as depressant. So lets discuss nicotine. Nicotine is a stimulate and a very deadly poison. Two drops of pure nicotine is more than enough to kill someone if it is administrated through the skin. Tobacco products don't have that much nicotine in them and products like the nicotine patch and gum have a lot more nicotine in each dose than a cigarette does. So the question is whether nicotine addictive or not. The answer is yes it is but it isn't the reason people are hooked on tobacco products. The main addictive property in tobacco products (at least in North America) is sugar. Each cigarette and cigar has 3% pure sugar in it, smokeless tobacco has even more.

Your Brain on Sugar

Sugar fuels every cell in the brain and influences brain chemicals, too. Overloading on sugary foods alters the brain receptors that regulate how much we eat. In laboratory studies, rats that binged on sugar had brain changes that mimicked those of drug withdrawal. In humans, just seeing pictures of milkshakes triggered brain activity similar to what's seen in drug addicts. When you eat cake, the sugar in that treat -- called a simple carbohydrate -- is quickly converted to glucose in your bloodstream. Your blood-sugar levels rise and spike when simple carbs are eaten alone, as when you grab a candy bar mid-afternoon. All simple carbs are absorbed quickly, most especially the processed, concentrated sugars found in syrup, soda, candy, and table sugar.

When you use tobacco

If you smoke, the sugar is immediately brought into your lungs at 1700 degrees F as smoke. The chemicals, particularly sugar, reach the brain ten seconds after the smoke is inhaled and remains active for 20-40 minutes. After reaching the brain, sugar affects changes and controls the specialized receptor cells (responsible for regulating the well-being, mood and memory) in the brain. This, in turn, changes the chemistry of the brain, which finally affects the smoker's mood. The secondary issue is nicotine addiction. The number of cell receptors for nicotine begin to increase as the smoker increases the amount they smoke, chew, or dip. When a person decides to give up tobacco, they are facing a physical response from every cell in their body that is craving nicotine. This is made worse by the sugar withdrawal, that in addition to giving flu-like symptoms, also makes the individual moody, have difficulty in focusing attention, critical, shaky, headaches, fatigue, depression, drowsiness, skin eruptions, and mucus or throat discomfort.

Using Hypnosis or Hypnotherapy to stop using tobacco
People started smoking for many different reasons and the reasons to want to stop are just varied. Some people can quit on their own. Why? That is a great question. If, as the cancer society, medical community, and the anti tobacco lobbyist promote, tobacco users are addicted to nicotine then these individuals should not be able to quit. Addictions (every addiction) have withdrawal symptoms that are highly unpleasant and often dangerous. Why is it that these few lucky individuals simply put down the tobacco and walk away never to return again? The answer is simple: Tobacco addiction isn't due to the nicotine but to the sugar. These few individuals that easily stop and never return have balanced their sugar levels and therefore, never suffer the sugar withdrawal that everyone else does. Most hypnotists treat tobacco use as a habit and simply give suggestions to break or replace the tobacco habit with another. This is known as transference and transference isn't good. This is why most people who stop using tobacco gain weight. They have transferred the sugar they received from the tobacco and now receive that sugar fix from eating or drinking alcohol. A hypnotherapist will most likely use a step-down method where the number of times tobacco is used is

slowly reduced, while adjusting the individual's food intake as well. This will balance the sugar levels, eliminating sugar withdrawal and minimizing nicotine withdrawal. The hypnotherapist can completely remove all withdrawal symptoms from any addiction; however, it is advised in certain cases, such as alcoholism and substance abuse, to work with both a medical doctor and a hypnotherapist. Tobacco dependance does not require a medical referral for a hypnotist or hypnotherapist to treat the client.

Weight Loss and Management

Weight loss in the United States is a 5 billion dollar a year industry. Unfortunately, it is an industry built on failure and guilt. The failure comes from the industry marketing that the way to lose weight is by caloric reduction, increase in cardio exercise as the method to lose those unwanted pounds. The truth is, this is a recipe to gain weight. In addition to weight gain, it also keeps the individual in the revolving door of losing weight, gaining even more weight than lost, returning to an even more caloric-reduced intake and more exercise, resulting in weight gain quickly as one resumes a normal diet.

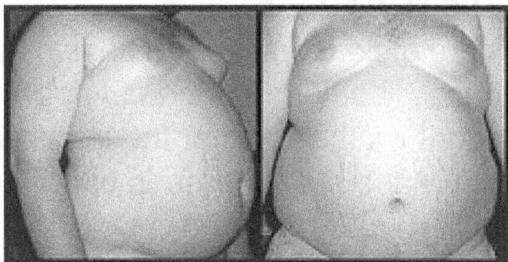

The leading weight-loss franchise stated in their own corporate documentation that the success factor of their program was 1%. If any corporation in the world produced a product that yielded a 1% success rate, they would go out of business.

According to the latest medical research all obesity can be traced to blood sugar and insulin imbalance. Insulin creates fat. Everyone within the medical community knows and understands this fact; however, to understand why this fact is being kept quiet one has to simply follow the money. Most hypnotists will simply read a script or will give suggestions to eat less. Let's discuss why this rarely works for the long term.

When I first meet with a client I take a full history including a hand written page where the client describes how long they have had a weight problem, what they have done in the past to resolve the weight problem, other medical issues that they may have, medication that is currently being taken, and I always do the hand test.

The Hand Test

Take a close look at these two hands. Do you see a difference? Look at the index finger. Longer index finger than ring finger on the hand of the left is a person who has hypoglycemia since birth (perhaps undetected) and the hand on the right is of a person who hasn't had hypoglycemia since birth but may have blood sugar issues now. Hypnotherapist **do not provide diagnosis** but just because we don't provide a diagnosis doesn't mean that we won't see something like this and strongly suggest that you visit your family doctor to discuss the possibility of this condition. Every time I see a

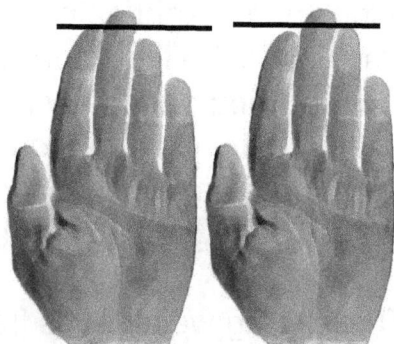

weight-loss client or a person who wants to stop using to-bacco, I always do the hand test. Why? Well for two reasons. First if the individual does have hypo-glycemia I have to han-dle their weight loss or tobacco cessation in a totally different way than if the person has no blood sugar issues. Secondly if the person does have hypoglycemia it always turns into type 2 diabetes if it remains untreated and I referral to their medical doctor may be in order.

If hypoglycemia is so bad then why hasn't my doctor told me about this? Well, again this question has two answers. First, your doctor has no way to treat this issue other than by diet. Second, there is no money in treating hypoglycemia. There is, however, a lot of money available if the condition turns into type 2 diabetes. Unfortunately the only way to test for hypo-glycemia is by an eight hour glucose tolerance test. Through the lobbying efforts of the American Diabetes Association, both insurance companies and doctors refuse to authorize glucose tolerance tests longer than one hour. Hypoglycemia will not show itself until hour 7 or 8. Therefore, hypoglycemia goes largely untreated in North America.

Every weight loss client begins the same way during the first four weeks of treatment when we are stabilizing their blood sugar. We are stopping the high peaks and low valleys and once we accomplish this the body is ready to release weight.

Eating 6 times a day
To understand successful weight loss we first must under-stand how the subconscious mind interprets things. It is the subconscious that determines when we eat and how much we

eat. The subconscious mind is very primitive and it acts and reacts to outside stimulus. It doesn't think about the stimulus it simply reacts to it. If I am feeling physically or mentally bad, the subconscious will give me a craving for sweet and salty foods. These foods will turn into sugar very quickly and immediately go to the brain. Once the sugars in the brain we receive a message of well being, relaxation or calmness, and happiness. The subconscious has two absolute truths. One, the subconscious wants to maintain the status quo. It hates change. Two, the subconscious is in total control of everything. So if the subconscious decides to do something, no matter how much will power you have (conscious mind is will power), no matter how much positive self talk you do (conscious controls self talk), at the end of the day you will be eating the cup cakes and other foods that break down into sugar quickly, if you are in physical or psychological pain.

The subconscious only understands feast or famine. If food is in abundance, the subconscious maintains the weight that it has set as normal and when famine comes the subconscious will divert everything to maintain the fat in the body. Fat is stored energy, and energy is life. That is what the subconscious understands and that is what our body is going to do. Thousands of years ago we were hunters and gatherers. We are designed to eat on the run, when food is available and where there is no food available our subconscious keeps us alive until food is available again. We must retrain the subconscious to understand that we are in a continual state of feasting. When we enter a weight-loss program we quite literally have to change the way we think, speak, and, most importantly, self talk.

The subconscious takes commands. It doesn't think, it doesn't evaluate, it acts and reacts. When we say for example "diet", the subconscious hears the word "die." The prime directive of the subconscious is self preservation, therefore, you saying that you are going to diet is telling the subconscious that you command it to die and that violates its prime directive of self preservation and therefore the diet command is nullified.

Severe caloric restriction
When we enter a diet plan such as Medifast, HCG, or others that limit the caloric intake to less than 1200 calories per day it forces our subconscious into famine mode. Yes, we will lose weight, of course we will; the subconscious is burning every calorie it is taking in and then making up the remainder of our physical requirement by burning fat; however, it will also burn lean muscle instead of fat until the last possible moment. Fat is the last line of defense for survival.

Once we have lost the weight we want and we resume a normal caloric intake, the subconscious kicks in and begins storing every calorie possible. The result is we regain the weight we have lost and then gain an extra 20 to 30 pounds more. This is the subconscious way of insuring that it will survive the next famine.

Medical doctors refer patients to me who have failed on every diet even medically supervised diets. My typical weight loss clients have between 100 to 500 pounds to lose. The program I have developed has been highly successful and the client sheds between 1 to 1.5 pounds of fat per week. Needless to say our program isn't fast; however, it works well and the client does not regain the weight.

The Neuro LapBand

A more drastic therapy is available for medically referred patients who have been advised to have gastric surgery. The gastric bypass, gastric Y, or lap band; however, the patient does not qualify for the surgery. Disqualification for this kind of surgery can be that the patient weighs too much to go under general anesthesia (if the patient weighs too much they may not recover from the anesthesia), or the patient has an intense fear of going under general anesthesia. Regardless of the reason the medical doctor believes that the patient's life is in danger without the operation but the patient will not have the procedure. Now we have created a therapy that emulates the gastric medical procedure without physically going though the surgical procedure and we achieve a higher success rate.

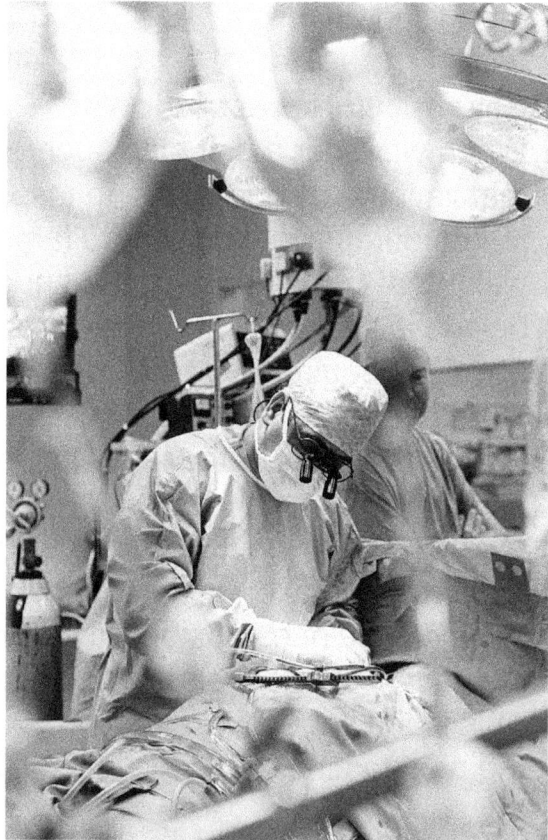

The Neuro LapBand combines behavior therapy while under hypnosis that allows the subconscious to go through the complete operation. The results: The clients lose the weight, are unable to eat normal amounts, and feel extreme tightness in the abdomen. This therapy was specifically designed for individuals who are at least 100 pounds or more over weight, have a Body Mass Index more than 40, and **must have a medical referral**. Our clients who have gone through the therapy report clearly recalling entering a hospital, hearing the medical staff, smelling the anesthesia, feeling pressure in the abdomen, and rolling down a hallway to the operating room. They also recall entering the operating room, seeing and hearing medical equipment, and hearing the medical staff talking to each other. None of this physically happened but it did happen in the subconscious and because the subconscious believes it really did happen, it releases the fat at the same rate as people who have had the medical procedure lose fat.

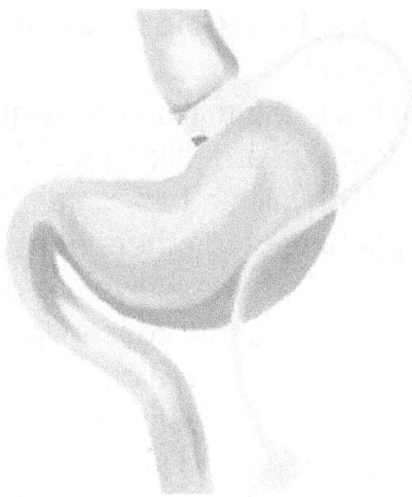

Addictions
Substance abuse

Why do people become addicted

This is the million dollar question, and the answer depends on who you are talking to. When I spoke with a medical doctor, the physician told me about an addictive gene that some people have and others don't. According to the doctor, once the gene is made active the person becomes addicted to tobacco, alcohol, food, prescription drugs, recreational drugs, soda, and the list goes on and on. When I speak to psychologists they tell me that individuals have physical and psychological addictions and it happens to everyone to a greater or lesser extent. He also told me that once someone is addicted they are always an addict and there is never a 100% recovery. When I have talked to people who advocate the various 12 step programs they tell me that we are all weak and that the addiction is beyond our control. They say we must turn to daily prayer and not to be too concerned about it if a client relapses into addiction because relapse is part of recovery. Often people who are in a 12 step program tend to have transference (the substitution of one addiction for another).

What I have found in my practice

I have never found any scientific evidence of an addictive gene and believe me I have reviewed the scientific data and medical reports and no matter how hard I look the evidence isn't there. In my work with clients who are addicts I have found that yes they can recover and they will not be addicted to whatever their addiction was any longer. I personally don't agree with many 12 step advocates. Don't misunderstand me, I believe that the 12 step program facilitators are caring and truly believe in what they are doing. They serve as a lifeline for thousands of people around the world at absolutely no charge. As a hypnotherapist I am only interested in resolving the issues. If a person comes to me for an addiction issue I immediately team up with a doctor and together we resolve the issue and the addiction goes away and does not return. In my opinion all addictions are caused by the individual attempting to self medicate to mask the symptoms of the issue or issues that's causing either physical or psychological pain. Let's take a look at the most common addiction that we have not already discussed.

Alcoholism

Alcohol is very common in our society and in most societies around the world; however, most of us drink as a social custom. We have a glass of wine to enhance the flavor of the dinner and we use alcohol to enhance our good time with friends and family.

The alcoholic doesn't drink to feel better or to get a "buzz' People who have alcohol dependency feel too much and drink to stop feeling anything at all. They may be in physical pain, mental pain, or a combination of the two. For me the interesting fact about alcoholism is that physical and emotional (analytical) become alcoholic for similar reasons. Physicals usually self medicate because they are manifesting physical symptoms from a psychological or emotional issue with rejection, or through peer pressure and the fear of being rejected if they do not participate. Emotionals (analytical) self medicate to quiet the mind from constantly analyzing and replaying events in their minds. Both reason are psychological yet manifest real physical symptoms that are disruptive enough to force the individual into use self medication to control the symptoms.

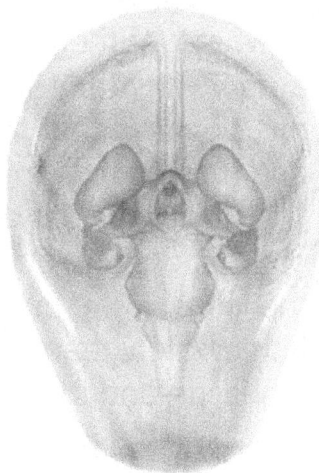

Addictions are complicated and require a team effort to successfully break the addiction: Allopathic (traditional western medicine) to monitor and make sure that the physical withdrawal of the substance does not create a situation where medical intervention is required. A hypnotherapist to helps the client to quickly resolve the issue that is triggering the self medication cycle. Additionally, the hypnotherapist should reduce or remove all withdrawal symptoms and pain. All therapy is individual rather than group and the results are amazing. Currently our statistic for individuals is a 96.5% success rate with no relapse in the five years we have began tracking our clients. 3.5% of the clients we have treated under this method have moved away and cannot be contacted.

Substance abuse other than alcohol

Prescription drugs is one of the most common addictions, and it may or may not surprise you to know that we are seeing children in elementary school who are addicted to their parents' or grandparents' prescriptions. All children below the age of 8 are highly physical. This means that the primary motivation to experiment is peer pressure and the fear of rejection. It also means that the child has not developed the critical cortex and the ability to look at possible long term consequences of their actions isn't possible.

Prescription medication is based on several factors, among them is the weight of the patient and physical or emotional symptoms that the patient is being treated for. One can immediately see the danger of an overdose of any prescription even over the counter medication taken by a child without adult supervision. The issue with children and prescription drugs is huge and unfortunately the media hasn't provided adequate coverage to inform us of how wide spread it really is. Prescription addiction is so common that even the emergency room doctors have a special code for it. Vitamin P which is code for Percocet also know as Tylox. Both of these brand names is for Oxycodone/Acetaminophen an oral pain medication that is very dangerous and possibly cause fatal liver failure. ER doctors often use the code vitamin P for a patient who has come to the emergency room specifically for Percocet also known as Oxycodone/Acetaminophen. Other prescription pain medications that are highly addictive are: Percodan, Talwinictive are: Vicodin, Laudanum, Morphine, Codeine, Methadone, Fentanyl Darvon, Demerol, Dilaudid, Orlaam, and OxyContin.

The addiction symptoms of these drugs are almost identical and include: Agitation, anxiety, muscle aches, increased tearing, insomnia, runny nose, sweating, yawning, abdominal cramping, diarrhea, dilated pupils, goose bumps and nausea and vomiting. The greatest issues with these specific drugs is that once the person is no longer addicted to the drug their tolerance to the drugs is greatly reduced and therefore, can overdose very easily even if prescribed by a physician.

This is one of the many reasons that rehab clinics and 12 step organizations preach that relapse is part of recovery. Without treating the underlying issue the subconscious will always return to whatever method of self medication that it has used in the past. Hypnotherapy can remove the issue quickly and greatly reduce the possibility of relapse.

(Side note) if the individual is in pain and his or her doctor will sign a medical referral stating that it will cause no harm if the hypnotherapist removes that specific pain the hypnotherapist may perform hypno-anesthesia and remove most or all of the pain the patient is feeling. This procedure does not stop the patient from feeling new pain, just the chronic pain that has already been identified.

The most common non-pain related prescription drugs that are abused: Adderall, Adderall XR, Concerta, Dexedrine, Focalin and Focalin XR, Metadate CD, Metadate ER, Methylin, Methylin ER, Ritalin, Ritalin SR, Ritalin LA, Vyvense, and Daytrana. These drugs are commonly over prescribed by "friendly doctors" to treat ADD/ADHD.

Most of these drugs are extremely high stimulants and the ones that are not stimulants have been specifically formulated to go to the brain and change the neurotransmitters. This is fine if you really do have ADD/ADHD; however, since there are no medical tests for ADD/ADHD "friendly doctors" who with nothing more than a letter from two teachers or a teacher and a school counselor will label the individual as ADD/ADHD and prescribe the drugs. ADD/ADHD is classified as a disorder with "NO CURE" and people who have been diagnosed with disorder(s) are expected to remain on this medication for life.

When I was teaching in a MBA program at the local university I was shocked to find that many of my students were buying these drugs on campus. The MBA program is demanding and these students felt that they needed the "edge" that these drugs provided. Unfortunately these students were more worried about making the cut for the next semester than the possible future health issues.

(Side note) an experienced hypnotherapist can easily remove the symptoms of ADD/ADHD from both children and adult in just a few sessions. Since the DSM says that

this disorder has "NO CURE" the medical doctors I have worked with have annotated in the patients medical records a "Misdiagnosis" and their patient does not have ADD/ADHD

Withdrawal symptoms from these drugs especially if it has been used regularly for a long time (longer than a few weeks) typically are severe tiredness, mood changes, depression, and sleep issues. In addition the individual may have heart palpitations and possible cardio failure.

Other Therapies
The hypnotherapist is specifically trained to perform other therapies. I thought this would be a great place to cover a few of them, to clarify   areas that hypnotherapist work in and hypnotist should avoid unless they have received extensive training in a classroom setting.

Hypnotherapy for Immune Disorders
The subconscious controls the immune system, and if the hypnotherapist has gone though this specific training they are qualified to work under the supervision of a physician in the following areas:

HIV/Aids, Asthma, Arthritis, Cancer, Chronic Fatigue Syndrome, Lupus, Multiple Sclerosis, and Fibromyalgia

This area of practice is called Psychoenuroimmunology which was recently established as a branch of medical science that studies and employs interactions between the mind (psyche)

the nervous system, and the immune system. This field of study is commonly know as Mind/Body medicine. The allopathic medical community has slowly embraced psychoenuroimmunology, more as a last resort rather than first choice. Referrals to hypnotherapists who are trained in psychoenuroimmunology are usually made instead of the traditional modalities, such when pharmaceuticals have failed.

Cancer patients often believe that they have been given a death sentence but this isn't true. I work with stage 4 cancer patients and even after the completion of chemotherapy (which kills the immune system) 94.7% of the stage 4 cancer patients I work with do not die. On the contrary their tumors shrink and disappear and they are totally cancer free at the completion of my therapeutic work with them. Regretfully, at this stage the hospitals in my area will not refer anyone to me who is less than stage 4 and only after all other treatment methods have failed.

The hypnotherapist that provides therapy to cancer patients MUST work directly with the patients oncologist. My experience is the oncologist may not understand why the therapy is working, but they can and will document that it is or isn't working as expected. If you are looking for a hypnotherapist and you are being treated, or have been treated for cancer make sure the hypnotherapist request a medical referral from your oncologist. If the hypnotherapist doesn't request one, keep looking you have not found your perfect hypnotherapist yet.

Asthma patients respond well to hypnotherapy where we specifically work on dilation of the bronchial tubes, dilation of the blood vessels, veins, and arteries in the lungs to allow more blood flow and the relaxation of all the muscles in the upper chest and abdomen. My asthma clients still visit their doctors on a regular basis; however, they rarely have an asthma attack or require the use of their inhaler. Even though my clients no longer suffer from asthma attacks or use the inhaler on a regular basis I always recommend they keep one with them at all times unless their doctor has told them they do not need to carry it any more. **A hypnotherapist or hypnotist should never tell a client to stop taking medication. Hypnotists and hypnotherapists do not prescribe drugs and they do not tell clients to discontinue drug therapy without the doctors written consent.**

Arthritis is classified as an auto immune disorder; however, the pain associated with the arthritis can be completely alleviated by the hypnotherapist using hypno anesthesia and teaching their client how to perform hypno anesthesia through self hypnosis to live pain free.

Lupus and fibromyalgia are both very painful disorders and prescription pain medication does not relieve the pain. Both are classified as auto immune disorders. My experience indicates that both of these disorders are caused by an imbalance in the individuals life and total lack of joy and happiness. Once the hypnotherapist has worked with the client to regain control in their life and reestablished joy and happiness by addressing the hostility and unresolved issues that the client has been carrying (often times for years) the pain and discomfort simply disappears.

Hypnotherapy for labor and childbirth has a distinguished history. The first documentation is from the 1920s in Russia. Dr. Platanov was well known for his hypno-obstetric success. For years this was the primary method of child birth in Russia and later in the United Soviet Socialist Republics (USSR). In 2007 the British Journal of Anesthesia (July 2007) did a comprehensive study and their conclusion was: "This report represents the most comprehensive review of the literature to date on the use of hypnosis for analgesia during childbirth. The meta-analysis shows that hypnosis reduces analgesia requirements in labor.

Apart from the analgesia and anesthetic effects possible in receptive subjects there are three other possible reasons why analgesic consumption during childbirth might be reduced when using hypnosis. First, teaching self hypnosis facilitates patient autonomy and sense of control. Secondly, the majority of participants are likely to be able to use hypnosis for relaxation, thus reducing apprehension that in turn may reduce analgesic requirements. Finally, the possible reduction in the need for pharmacological augmentation of the labor when hypnosis is used for childbirth, may be minimize the incidence of uterine hyperstimulation and the need for epidural analgesia."

Using hypno-childbirth provides the safest and most natural way for an individual to bring a child into the world. The new mom is relaxed and calm. The new dad, if he is in the delivery room, is also very relaxed and calm even though the lights are bright, there are strange smells, lots of equipment and activity by the OBGYN and staff. The OBGYN doctors that I have worked with love this method because they do not need to introduce chemicals into the moms body that will have an effect on the child and there are absolutely no side effects to this method of child birth except lots of smiles and laughter.

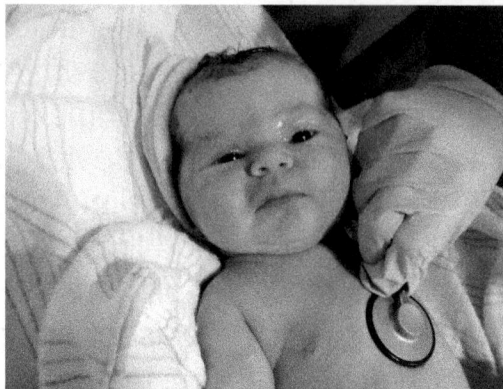

Lamaze method of childbirth was created by Dr. Fernand Lamaze when he went to Russia to observe Dr. Platanov and his work. After observing Dr. Platanov for two weeks Dr. Lamaze brought back to France this idea of focusing on the breathing and relaxation. Unfortunately Dr. Lamaze didn't understand hypnosis or hypno-anesthesia so the Lamaze method really doesn't work well for most people

Hypnotherapy for PTSD is the most effective method of treatment. It is fast, requires no medication, and removes all negative symptoms of PTSD. Traditionally, we think of PTSD as a disorder that only combat veterans, first responders (firefighters and police officers) have but it. I have seen children as young as 5 who had all of the textbook symptoms of PTSD. Anyone can have PTSD at any age.

Why traditional therapy for PTSD doesn't work
The traditional therapy for PTSD is talk therapy (psychoanalysis (performed by a psychiatrist), psychotherapy (individual and group performed by a psychologist, LPC, MFT, D.Ed.), and drug therapy (performed by an MD or DO, or psychiatrist).

The reason that these traditional therapies don't work is because talk therapy is based on the idea of repressed memories that cannot be recalled. PTSD is memories which cannot be forgotten or put in the past, that stimulate the fight/flight response at inappropriate times. We have all heard the story of the combat veteran who is working and suddenly has a flash back to being in combat and believes that all of their coworkers are the enemy. Yes, that does happen on occasion; however, the more common symptom is sudden outburst of anger, crying, confusion, physical shaking, distance, lack of empathy, loss of time (not showing up to functions or appointment or arriving late), feeling totally alone, and sometimes disorientation (totally confused on where they are or how they got there). The only assistance a medical doctor can offer (and this includes psychiatrists) is drug therapy. Drug therapy masks the outward appearance of these symptoms, but mostly they make the individual lethargic, unable to focus, and much of the time unable to remain gainfully employed.

Talk therapy only increases the anger and frustration. Again all talk therapy is based on repressed memories. The idea of talk therapy is that, over time the subconscious will let some of these repressed memories come out and then the therapist can guide the conversation toward those memories and deal with the underlying issues. Sounds great doesn't it? Well, with PTSD there are no repressed memories. All of the memories keep coming out, and the individual continues to mentally relive the situation. As the individual attempts to adapt, the therapist rehashes the events that caused the memories in the first place and thereby reinforces the memories, making them stronger and increasing the fight/flight response in the individual. The result is increased inappropriate behavior which this leads to either an increase in the dose of medication or additional medication, this leads to an increase feeling of worthlessness and inability to function in society, leading to depression and more inappropriate behavior, and the circle of treatment continues without end.

Hypnotherapy and PTSD actually have a long history. In World War I PTSD was called Shell Shock or battle fatigue. Different names for the exact same disorder. Hypnosis and hypnotherapy was the only thing used, simply because the typical drugs used today were not created back then. Psychiatrists back then actually used hypnotherapy on a regular basis and they achieved the results they were looking for. Suddenly patients who had no physical injuries yet their body manifested physical symptoms such as paralysis, or an inability to speak were able to walk and talk again.

By the time World War II erupted we began seeing a new type of situation. Now combat troops were given drugs to increase their alertness while lessening their sleep cycles. Many of the drugs that the United States forces were given are still classified; however, we do know that the German combat troops were being given a brand new drug called Pervitin, a stimulant known today as speed. The Nazis continued working on stronger stimulants that would eliminate the need for sleep for 24 hours or more, increase the individual's self esteem and focus. The answer was D-IX; this contained five milligrams of Eukodal (a morphine based painkiller) and three milligrams of Pervitin. A new drug was issued to German troops called methamphetamine and these were used by the army and air force between April and July of 1940. This new drug was banned in 1941 under the Opium Law; however over 10 million tablets were sent to the soldiers later that year. In addition to the drugs, alcohol consumption was encouraged. Now we know what a deadly combination this was, but at the time this was the best that medical minds could come up with and the medical community declared this to be safe.

Hypnotherapy was used to treat the individual symptoms of PTSD but very little was done for the drug abuse.

After World War II, American soldiers were receiving a different kind of therapy. It was drug therapy that placed the individual in a highly suggestible state where a doctor untrained in hypnotherapy would make suggestions and the physical symptoms magically disappeared; however, not the mental effects. World War II veterans self-medicated themselves with the drug of choice, alcohol.

The Vietnam War introduced a new drug for soldiers that were fighting a war that psychologically they were not prepared to fight, this drug was marijuana. Marijuana is a depressant and would allow the soldiers to calm down and move out of the fight/flight syndrome that all combat troops are in while they are in the field. Marijuana didn't make the soldier more alert, on the contrary it slowed down their response to danger. Marijuana didn't affect military operations because the soldiers only used it during non-combat situations. Vietnam was the first war in which American forces met with civilian combatants. Traditionally women and children are not combatants and combatants wear uniforms. This was not the case in Vietnam and the psychological damage to American soldiers was astounding. Returning soldiers with PTSD flooded the United States; unfortunately the civilian medical community didn't know how to deal with PTSD and the military (Veterans Hospitals) used standard drug therapy and talk therapy with very poor results. Again self-medication by the individual increased and they returned to drugs of choice in Vietnam, marijuana and alcohol.

Civilians with PTSD began to rise with family members because of all of the issues these returning soldiers had, flash backs, sudden violent outbursts, and suicide. PTSD is caused by memories being burned into the brain with Adrenaline. Adrenaline is the fight or flight response of the adrenal gland. When the body releases adrenaline, it also releases dopamine which is a natural pain killer. This creates the "numbing" of personal emotional feelings towards a situation.

The hypnotherapist who has been specifically trained to use hypnotherapy with PTSD patients can quickly eliminate all physical and emotional issues that have been so pronounced in every area of his or her life. Once therapy has been completed, there is no need for continued drug therapy and additional talk therapy and the mental health professional or medical doctor who reviews the hypnotherapist results often signs off on the case with decreasing check up visits. The result is no more anger outburst, no need for the continued use of the drugs, the ability to return to being emotionally responsive to a family, and return to the work place without fear of relapse.

Hypnotherapy and the Legal System
Working with attorneys, police, and the court system is challenging but very interesting. Attorneys use hypnotherapist to increase their own personal performance in a court room situation. Witness preparation is vital to any court appearance. The witness must appear to be honest, and forthcoming to a jury. Hypnotherapists work with witnesses to insure that they remain calm when being examined and cross examined.

Police and prosecuting attorneys use hypnotherapists to regress victims. Now before we go any further, testimony from a person who has been hypnotized to remember is not admissible in a court of law. Here is the procedure to make the testimony admissible. The police, with the prosecuting attorney in attendance, observe the hypnotherapist place the witness or victim into hypnosis. The hypnotherapist then regresses the witness or victim to the day in question while being placed in either a movie theatre or some other safe place where they can observe the event of the day without any emotional attachment.

After the events have been observed the hypnotherapist brings the witness or victim out of hypnosis and then the police or prosecuting attorney begins to question the witness or victim. The witness or victim will have total recall of the event, including the most insignificant detail. The witness or victim is not under the influence of hypnosis when the statement or interview is conducted, and because no questions were asked while the witness or victim was under hypnosis the full testimony is admissible.

Medical Hypnotherapy is a challenging and exciting area of specialization. The medical hypnotherapist works directly with medical doctors and their patients in the areas of pre and post medical procedure, sexual dysfunction, crisis intervention, hospice care, pain free labor and child birth, immune disorders, pain management, cognitive behavior therapy, dream therapy, physical performance, remove stroke symptoms, ADD/ADHD, and autism. This is only a sampling of areas that the medical hypnotherapist work in.

Past Life Regression and Future Progression is one of the most exciting areas of hypnotherapy because it combines pure science with the spiritual. Used prominently for entertainment purposes past life regression does serve a therapeutic purpose as well; however, past life regression should only be practiced on an individual client, NEVER IN A GROUP SETTING and never with any client who has not specifically requested a past life regression or a future progression.

One very common question I am often asked is "Can any harm come from a past life regression or a future life progression?" No, provided that the hypnotherapist performing the regression or progression is properly trained. In a past life regression we usually take the client all of the way through the life and this includes the death experience for that life. Some people want to experience it and feel everything, others want to experience but not experience the pain associated with the death experience, while others only wish to observe it. If the person taking one through the past life regression isn't well-trained then it is possible that the client could feel some panic, discomfort, and fear as they experience the death experience without being properly prepared. This is why it is never wise to conduct past life regression in a group setting. It is possible that some people could have abreactions or experience pain and panic from the sessions not being conducted correctly.

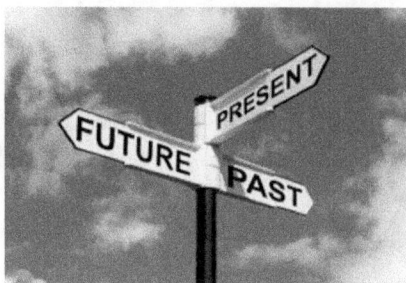

In well over 500 past life regressions, I have only had one individual who was regressed to someone who could be independently verified as having lived and all of the details of the individuals life were completely accurate. In this specific case I and some of my associates spent approximately 2000 hours researching the information that the client related to us while under hypnosis. Even then the client's past life was not recorded in history books; but verification through family records that were obtained through ancestry.com, which lead to conversations with descendants of the person our client believe he is a reincarnation of.

Future life progression is used when a client is in conflict. Future life progression allows the client to view every choice they have and to track every aspect of that choice with its outcome. Once the client comes out of hypnosis they now have more information to process before they make a final decision. I have performed over 300 future life progressions and have observed positive results after every session.

About the Author

David Newman, D.Sc., is a certified hypnotherapist, the director of RoseHeart Hypnotherapy Success Centers, Inc., the voice of Success Talk radio show, writer, lecturer and presenter.

In 2006 David left his consulting business to devote his full time efforts in the field of Hypnotherapy. Dr. Newman graduated the Hypnosis Motivation Institute the first accredited school in the United State. Since, graduation Dr. Newman has continued to practice hypnotherapy full time while conducting research and perfect therapies in medical hypnosis, ADD/ADHD, autism, PTSD, and cancer.

David has created specific therapies for PTSD, ADD/ADHD, and Neuro LapBand weight loss for individuals who have been advised to have gastric bypass, gastric Y, or Lap Band operations.

David may be reached at his office (888)604-9997 ex 3

Dr. David Newman, D.Sc., C. Ht
RoseHeart Hypnotherapy Success Centers, Inc
609 Clark Avenue
Jefferson City, Missouri 65101

websites http://www.mohyp.com
http://www.drdavidnewman.com or
http://www.neurolapband.com
Twitter: @drdavidnewman

Afterward

Throughout this book I have been careful to address every topic from an impersonal, scientific, and totally objective point of view. I would like to talk about what it is like to be a practicing hypnotherapist.

In all of my speaking engagements I always ask this question: We are taught that we are physical beings on earth in an attempt to have a spiritual experience, but what if this is wrong? What if, we are spiritual beings on earth to have physical experiences? Wow, that just became a major game changer. Suddenly we are instantly moved from being a victim who has no control over what life throws at them and transported to an active participant who is in control of what happens to us and how we respond to those events.

If we are spiritual beings in human form, it is logical to presume that we have special abilities hidden deeply within us. Science has proven that our subconscious mind is similar to a super computer except our subconscious is infinitely more powerful. We can find references to the power of our mind in ancient writings "as a man thinks so he is," "if you believe it is done, it is done," and "If you want to change your life, change your thought." Some of those quotes may sound familiar to you, I took them from some of the most holy, and profound writings from around the world.

Science has proven that the subconscious controls every aspect of our body that we don't consciously think about, but Dr. Kappas developed a theory "is based on the belief that the subconscious mind is a goal machine, dedicated and driven for the fulfillment of a programmed path. All of the events of our lives, including "luck", both good and bad, is a manifestation of the energy that emanates from our subconscious mind as it continually strives to fulfill the agenda for which it is programmed. In all of my studies and classes that I have, the theory of Dr. Kappas is absolutely correct.

As a practicing hypnotherapist I have the honor of witnessing miracles happening every day. These are not supernatural miracles although sometime they seem like they are.

The hypnotherapist is a subconscious behaviorist. We have spent our lives in classes, seminars, internships, research clinics, and in actual full time practice. The trained hypnotherapist doesn't use "scripts," "pre-recorded sessions," or simply pop in a CD to place a person into hypnosis and conduct the session. Many hypnotist do. Hypnotherapist don't perform "group" hypnosis. We are like all other medical professionals, we work with
one client at a time, and we are paid to achieve the desired results.

Peter G. Moore, M.D., Ph.D, of UC Davis Department of Anesthesiology and Pain Medicine said: "all modern pharmaceutical pain medicine are in many ways a placebo. That is some pharmaceuticals work of some people and not on others, some will work on children, others only work for adults. If a pharmaceutical is not a placebo it would work on every person that it is administered to. This brings us up to hypnoanesthesia. "I cannot explain how it work, but we have conducted

studies using PED scans of patients in chronic pain. The results were amazing, when we used standard pain medication (nerve block) and we could clearly see that the area of the brain that registerers discomfort were not receiving a signal; however, when we placed the patient under hypnosis with a hypnotherapist trained in hypnoanesthesia, we could watch the area that registerers discomfort in the brain dim and become inactive and the area of the brain that registers pleasure become active. There is no question that something real was going on and while I am not able to explain it, I know that it works. In my opinion every medical doctor should be trained in hypnoanesthesia as well as standard pharmacology."
Wow, total pain relief is it a miracle? No it is the subconscious in action.

Shaye J.D. Cohen, Ph.D., mentions several time in his class on Culture and Belief that he teaches at Harvard, "every culture, every society, in every age certain individual knew how to use the subconscious mind to manifest healing, success, and well being." In the Hebrew and Christian beliefs we often refer to these people as Prophets. Dr. Cohen further said B"Jesus told his followers that if you believe you will work even greater miracles than I have done."

Before modern medicine there was hypnotherapist that provided cures. Before modern psychology and psychotherapy there was the hypnotherapist providing treatment and resolving the issues. Before the introduction of chemical anesthesia there was the hypnotherapist that provided anesthesia for medical procedures. My final word of advice. There are thousands of people who claim to be hypnotist or hypnotherapist who prey of the uniformed. They all have elaborate stories of their training and successes; however, they don't hold up when placed under the bright light of scrutiny. Now you have the tools to inquire, verify, interview, and select The Perfect Hypnotherapist. I wish you the best of success!

Letters From Actual Clients and Medical Professionals about Hypnotherapy

I found Dr. Newman by accident. My husband and I were at wits-end because of behavior issues with my two daughters. They were always fighting with much resentment directed towards my husband and me. We spend time and lots of money going to family therapist, behavior therapist, medical doctors, drug therapy (for the girls) and nothing worked. I heard Dr. Newman on National Public Radio. After the first visit we saw an immediate change in behavior and study habits. Between the second and third visit both of the girls had dramatically raised their grade point average at school, and the fighting between them and disrespect that had been directed towards my husband and me was gone. This was a real miracle that happened before our eyes. We recommend hypnotherapy to our family and friends all the time.

Julie

At the age of 18 I was diagnosed with Raynaud's Phenomenon (Raynaud's Phenomenon is a circulatory condition that affects the fingers, toes, ears, and nose). In essence I was always cold and I was commonly called "the walking dead" because I was so cold. My medical doctor prescribed drug therapy that was minimally successful. I was introduced to Dr. Newman and hypnotherapy. After my initial sessions my hands stayed warm for two days. After the second session my hand remain warm and comfortable. During my third session Dr. Newman focused on my feet and to my amazement they are also warm and comfortable. My coworkers and family have noticed the difference and I no longer take the prescriptions that my doctor had prescribed. When I visited my doctor and he shook my hand he immediately noticed the difference and asked me what I was doing that was different (since his treatments had been ineffective) I told him hypnotherapy and he said "the mind is a powerful thing."

Carol

I am a VP of Operations for a local TV station. I have all sorts of stress related issues and illness. I told Dr. Newman that I am a walking pharmacy taking six different pharmaceutical regiments a day, every day for years. After my clinical intake with Dr. Newman, I immediately noticed that I felt much better, my mind was sharper, and my body felt good. I haven't felt good for years. I cannot explain what happen but something very positive happened during that session.

Susan

I was referred to Dr. Newman, by my orthopedic surgeon because one of the vertebrae in my spine crushed after my back stabilization surgery; for the next five years I didn't leave my house, or my bed unless it was absolutely necessary. I saw Dr. Newman twice. After the first session my pain went from a

10+ down to a 2. After the second session my pain went down from a 2 to a 0. Now I can walk without pain, clean my house, and make dinner. This was an absolute god send for me.

Rita

I am a licensed and practicing psychologist. I have and will continue to recommend the hypnotherapy of Dr. Newman to my patients that have leveled out and are not progressing further in their therapy. I have observed first hand my patients making a full recovery and not needing additional therapy after a few short sessions with Dr. Newman. I whole heartily endorse hypnotherapy by a well trained and seasoned hypnotherapist

Dr. J. Sennott, Psychologist

I was diagnosed with stage 3 cancer and I was going though chemotherapy which is painful. I was referred to Dr. Newman by my oncologist because of his work with cancer and pain management. I am familiar with hypnosis but had always found it ineffective until I met with Dr. Newman. I have never experienced anything as profound as what he is able to do. My pain immediately dropped to a level of 1. I am totally amazed.
Patrick

I am a licensed psychologist associated with a local hospital. I met Dr. Newman because one of my patients had head of him and wanted to try hypnotherapy. I am certified in hypnosis and NLP but I have found them to be totally ineffective and I have never been able to get the desired results. I told my patent to hold off and to let me "check him out."

I made an appointment with Dr. Newman for a clinical intake. I was surprised when he performed a handwriting analysis and the information he drew from that sample was amazing to say the least. It was like he had known me for years and he showed deep insight to my referring issue. Dr. Newman placed me into hypnosis though a process that I was totally unfamiliar with but is highly effective. I was and remain amazed. I have referred many patients to him and he has always delivered the results that I was looking for in a fraction of the time it would have taken me to achieve though typical therapeutic modalities that we use in the hospital.
Linda, LPC

My sons teachers told me that I had to take my son to a doctor because he has ADD/ADHD. The teacher insisted that my son needed to be placed on medication. My son said the drugs made him feel funny, tired, and he didn't want to do anything except stop taking it. I thought we would try something else. I went to Dr. Newman, and he "removed the symptoms of ADD/ADHD." I am not sure what he did exactly, but the results were almost immediate and was so successful that my doctor took him off of the medication. My son is healthy, happy, a great student, and cooperative.
Kim

I lost my husband a few years ago and since that date I have bounced in and out of depression. I had been institutionalized several times because my depression moved me to attempt to take my own life. My psychiatrist only wanted to prescribe drugs that didn't work. My psychiatrist referred me to a psychologist after I was discharged from the hospital and my psychologist said I would have to stay on drugs for the rest of my life. I didn't want to continue to take the drugs, and I was frustrated that I couldn't get the answer to the question of why can't I let go and move forward with my life.

I found Dr. Newman and hypnotherapy though a friend of mine and I mentioned it to my psychologist. He asked me who the hypnotherapist was and when I told him he said "yes, he is very good. I will write a referral for you, but you still need to see me for a while." After my first session with Dr. Newman, I felt better, and slowly we began moving though all of the hurt, anger, and thousands of other emotions that I didn't ever realize were creating my situation. Dr. Newman worked closely with my psychologist and my psychologist was surprised at how quickly I was improving. Hypnotherapy did for me what drugs and my psychologist couldn't do. It gave me peace, joy, and the ability to look forward to a bright future. Candi

When I came to see Dr. Newman I was a mess. My career was going nowhere, my marriage was on the rocks, and I had difficulty focusing on anything for longer than a few minutes. Dr. Newman taught be about my subconscious life script and how to rewrite it. Hypnotherapy restored my confidence, happiness, and ambition. Because I live in Australia we never met in person, but though video sessions. After four session I am a new man with a bright future. Colin

Dearest David,

I just wanted to say thank you so much for this program. As you know, I am an OBGYN Doctor here in the Atlanta area. I have the joy of playing a large role of bringing life into the world. I have been in practice for over 20 years and find my field of expertise quite interesting. I have seen women who go through 30 hours of labor and others who walk in the door ready to deliver after only an hour of contractions.

Every woman who comes into the labor room is nervous and excited. Some times the nervous and excitement can cause a longer labor and make the delivery more painful. It can also cause stress on the baby.

I had been searching for a way to help these new mothers relax and lessen the discomfort of this process. I talked to my sister Kitty O'Malley who is also in the medical field and she told me about what your relaxation MP3 and what it had done for her after only one listening session. I told her that I would give it a try but I was not going to get excited about it until I see if it works. I spoke with you and asked for the download. Thankfully you sent it right away.

The first person I thought I would try this on was my husband Steve. He is also a Doctor and shares a practice with me and two other doctors. We had been changing many things in our office and converting to an updated computer system.We were having to train our whole staff. It was quite frustrating for Steve as he is the one who did most of the training. He would come home and get angry at the littlest thing. I had him sit down and listen to the MP3. With in minutes, my husband was a new man. He got up and kissed me and said thank you. He had not done that in a long time.

I began using this program in the labor room nearly two months ago. I knew that this would help the mothers in labor but I had no idea that I would see such a change in the fathers as well. When they first arrive, mom is nervous but dad is scared to death. The father always tries to play the tough guy but it is so easy to see that he is terrified. After using the program for a week, I did a quick study on how this was affecting the families. I was amazed at how the labor coaches were calm which made the expectant mother calm. I must say that I love how this program works. We use it in the office and at home on a regular basis.

Thank you so much David for sending this our way. Our patients are more relaxed, my husband is less frustrated and I am breathing easier. I am very interested in more information on your services. Please send me everything you have on this subject.

Thank you,

Casandra O'Malley MD/OBGYN

To request your free MP3 via email please send an email to clinic@mohyp.com or go to http://www.mohyp.com and go to contact us and request us to send the 5 Minute Miracle. It will be sent to though a reply email. Rose-Heart Hypnotherapy Success Centers, Inc. does not sell, lease, give, or release any information or email addresses from anyone who writes to us.

Forms and Illustrations

BODY SYNDROMES

The theory of **Body Syndromes** is based on the principle that whenever an *emotional trauma* is present, a corresponding *physical reaction* will take place. These physical reactions, called *body syndromes*, will in turn reflect the cause of the emotional trauma according to the area(s) of the body that becomes affected by pain. pressure, or tension.

Below are the 5 Body Syndromes. Please pick from a scale of 1 to 10 to rate each area and place that number along the side of the model.

(10) the highest rating	(5) average rating	(1) the lowest rating

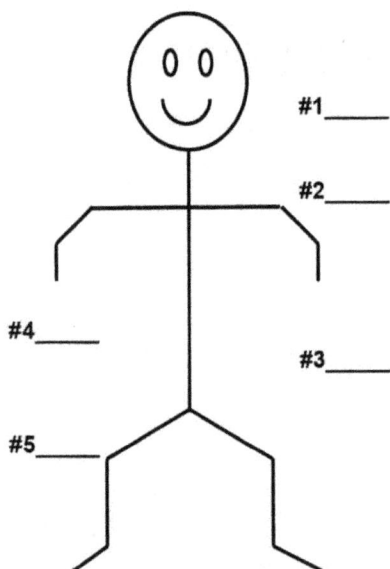

SYNDROME #1: "Crying"
Areas from the top of the head down to the solar plexus of the chest. This represents the inability to make decisions.

SYNDROME #2: "Responsibility"
Areas from the shoulders to the upper back. This often represents taking on too much responsibility or neglecting /not accepting it.

SYNDROME #3: "Frustration/Guilt"
Areas from the stomach, groin, hips to lower back. This represents sexual frustration or feelings of guilt for actions or behavior.

SYNDROME #4: "Fight/Reaching"
Area of the arms, hands and fingers. This represents what you are holding on to, not letting go or pushing away in your life.

SYNDROME #5: "Flight/Running"
Area from the thighs to the feet and toes. This represents a need of wanting to escape or run away from a current situation.

#1_____

#2_____

#4_____

#3_____

#5_____

THE THEORY OF MIND

"How Hypnosis Works with the Conscious and Subconscious Mind"

The Hand Test
Showing
Blood Sugar Issues

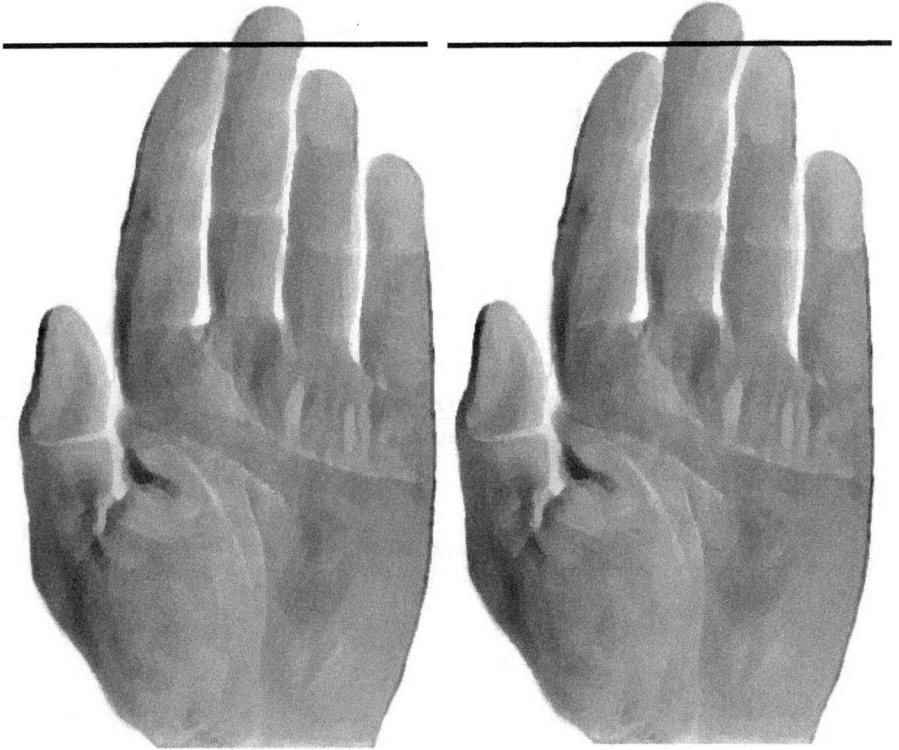

Hand showing Hypoglycemia   Normal Hand

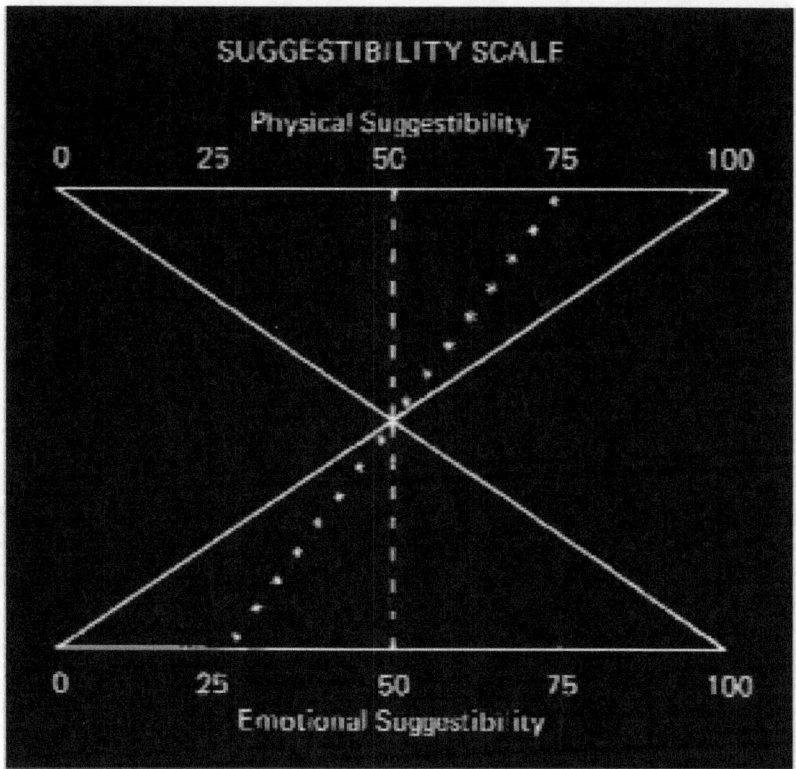

SUGGESTIBILITY SCALE

Physical Suggestibility

0   25   50   75   100

Emotional Suggestibility

0   25   50   75   100

Scoring Instructions

1. For both questionnaires score 10 points for yes answers for question 1 and 2.

2. For all remaining questions 5 points for each yes answer.

3. Total the number of points for each yes answer on sheet 1

4. Total the number of points for each yes answer on sheet 2

5. Add the totals for sheet 1 and sheet 2

6. Find the score for sheet 1 on the short side of the score sheet

7. Find the score for both sheets on the long side of the score sheet.

8. Follow the grid and where the row from sheet 1 intercepts the volume from the total of sheet 1 and 2 that will give you the percentage of physical you are.

9. Subtract this score from 100 and you get the percentage of Emotional (analytical)

Important Note: If you are a member of an ethnic family or culture subtract 10% from the physical score. Ethnic score higher on the physical suggestibility and a statical correction should be made

Suggestibility Questionnaire #1

1	Have you ever walked in your sleep during your adult life?	YES NO
2	As a teenager, did you feel comfortable expressing your feelings to one or both of your parents	YES NO
3	Do you have a tendency to look directly into a person's eyes and/or move closely to them when discussing an interesting subject?	YES NO
4	Do you feel that most people, when you first meet them, are uncritical of your appearance?	YES NO
5	In a group situation with people you have just met, would you feel comfortable drawing attention to yourself by initiating a conversation?	YES NO
6	Do you feel comfortable holding hands or hugging someone you are in a relationship with in front of other people?	YES NO
7	When someone talks about feeling warm physically, do you begin to feel warm also?	YES NO
8	Do you tend to occasionally tune out when someone is talking to you because you are anxious to come up with your side, and, at times, not hear what the other person said?	YES NO
9	Do you feel that you learn and comprehend better by seeing and /or reading than by hearing?	YES NO
10	In a new class or lecture situation, do you usually feel comfortable asking questions in front of the group?	YES NO
11	When expressing your ideas, do you find it important to relate all the details leading up to the subject so the other person can understand it completely?	YES NO
12	Do you enjoy relating to children?	YES NO
13	Do you find it easy to be at ease and comfortable with your body movements, even when faced with unfamiliar people and circumstances?	YES NO
14	Do you prefer reading fiction rather than non-fiction?	YES NO
15	If you were to imagine sucking on a sour, bitter, juicy, yellow lemon, would your mouth water?	YES NO
16	If you feel that you deserve to be complimented for something well done, do you feel comfortable if the compliment is given to you in front of other people?	YES NO
17	Do you feel that you are a good conversationalist?	YES NO
18	Do you feel comfortable when complimentary attention is drawn to your physical body or appearance?	YES NO

102

Suggestibility Questionnaire #2

1	Have you ever awakened in the middle of the night and felt that you could not move your body and/or talk?	YES	NO
2	As a child, did you feel that you were more affected by your parents tone of voice, than by what they actually said?	YES	NO
3	If someone you are associated with talks about a fear that you have experienced before, do you have a tendency to have an apprehensive or fearful feeling also?	YES	NO
4	After having an argument with someone, do you have a tendency to dwell on what you could or should have said?	YES	NO
5	Do you tend to occasionally tune out when someone is talking to you and, therefore, do not hear what was said because your mind drifts to something totally unrelated?	YES	NO
6	Do you sometimes desire to be complimented for a job well done, but feel embarrassed or uncomfortable when complimented?	YES	NO
7	Do you often have a fear or dread of not being able to carry on a conversation with someone you've just met?	YES	NO
8	Do you feel self-conscious when attention is drawn to your physical body or appearance?	YES	NO
9	If you had a choice, would you rather avoid being around children most of the time?	YES	NO
10	Do you feel that you are not relaxed or loose in body movements, especially when faced with unfamiliar people or circumstances?	YES	NO
11	Do you prefer reading non-fiction rather than fiction?	YES	NO
12	If someone describes a very bitter taste, do you have difficulty experiencing the physical feeling of it?	YES	NO
13	Do you generally feel that you see yourself less favorably than others see you?	YES	NO
14	Do you tend to feel awkward or self-conscious initiating touch (holding hands, kissing, etc.) with someone you are in a relationship with, in front of other people?	YES	NO
15	In a new class or lecture situation, do you usually feel uncomfortable asking questions in front of the group, even though you may desire further explanation?	YES	NO
16	Do you feel uneasy if someone you have just met, looks you directly in the eyes when talking to you, especially if the conversation is about you?	YES	NO
17	In a group situation with people you have just met, would you feel uncomfortable drawing attention to yourself by initiating a conversation?	YES	NO
18	If you are in a relationship, or are very close to someone, do you find it difficult or embarrassing to verbalize your love for them?	YES	NO

The Perfect Hypnotherapist.

COMBINED SCORE #1 AND #2

Score #1	50	55	60	65	70	75	80	85	90	95	100	105	110	115	120	125	130	135	140	145	150	155	160	165	170	175	180	185	190	195	200
100											100	95	91	87	83	80	77	74	71	69	67	65	63	61	59	57	56	54	53	51	50
95										100	95	90	86	83	79	76	73	70	68	66	63	61	59	58	56	54	53	51	50	49	48
90									100	95	90	86	82	78	75	72	69	67	64	62	60	58	56	55	53	51	50	49	47	46	45
85								100	94	89	85	81	77	74	71	68	65	63	61	59	57	55	53	52	50	49	47	46	45	44	43
80							100	94	89	84	80	76	73	70	67	64	62	59	57	55	53	52	50	48	47	46	44	43	42	41	40
75						100	94	88	83	79	75	71	68	65	63	60	58	56	54	52	50	48	47	45	44	43	42	41	39	38	38
70					100	93	88	82	78	74	70	67	64	61	58	56	54	52	50	48	47	45	44	42	41	40	39	38	37	36	35
65				100	93	87	81	76	72	68	65	62	59	57	54	52	50	48	46	45	43	42	41	39	38	37	36	35	34	33	33
60			100	92	86	80	75	71	67	63	60	57	55	52	50	48	46	44	43	41	40	39	38	36	35	34	33	32	32	31	30
55		100	92	85	79	73	69	65	61	58	55	52	50	48	46	44	42	41	39	38	37	35	34	33	32	31	31	30	29	28	28
50	100	91	83	77	71	67	63	59	56	53	50	48	45	43	42	40	38	37	36	34	33	32	31	30	29	29	28	27	26	26	25
45	90	82	75	69	64	60	56	53	50	47	45	43	41	39	38	36	35	33	32	31	30	29	28	27	26	26	25	24	24	23	23
40	80	73	67	62	57	53	50	47	44	42	40	38	36	35	33	32	31	30	29	28	27	26	25	24	24	23	22	22	21	21	20
35	70	64	58	54	50	47	44	41	39	37	35	33	32	30	29	28	27	26	25	24	23	23	22	21	21	20	19	19	18	18	18
30	60	55	50	46	43	40	38	35	33	32	30	29	27	26	25	24	23	22	21	21	20	19	19	18	18	17	17	16	16	15	15
25	50	45	42	38	36	33	31	29	28	26	25	24	23	22	21	20	19	19	18	17	17	16	16	15	15	14	14	14	13	13	13
20	40	36	33	31	29	27	25	24	22	21	20	19	18	17	17	16	15	15	14	14	13	13	13	12	12	11	11	11	11	10	10
15	30	27	25	23	21	20	19	18	17	16	15	14	14	13	13	12	12	11	11	10	10	10	9	9	9	9	8	8	8	8	8
10	20	18	17	15	14	13	13	12	11	11	10	10	9	9	8	8	8	7	7	7	7	6	6	6	6	6	6	5	5	5	5
5	10	9	8	8	7	7	6	6	6	5	5	5	5	4	4	4	4	4	4	3	3	3	3	3	3	3	3	3	3	3	3

Score # 1

Final Thoughts

After reading this book I am pleased to tell you that you now know more about hypnosis and hypnotherapy than just about any medical doctor, psychiatrist, psychologist, and unfortunately hypnotist or hypnotherapist. This is the sad fact; however, the good news is you are now well armed and are ready to find, interview, and select your perfect hypnotherapist. I would like to offer you a bit of advice. Please do not go to a "traveling hypnotist, or hypnotherapist. No matter what their ads may say they are not "world famous" and they may never have gone though any formal training of any kind.

My advice to you is NEVER get to a stage hypnotist for therapy. There is a huge difference between entertainment and therapy. Never, work with a hypnotist or a hypnotherapist whose training cannot be verified by you. Take the time to do a bit of research. Google search each candidate that you are considering, call the association that granted them certification. If you are unable to speak to a real person, or if they cannot give you specifics about the individual, take a pass and keep looking. Finally, search for books that they have written, articles that they have written and have been published. During your interview the hypnotist or hypnotherapist should answer every question that you may ask, if you don't understand their answer, tell them that, and make them rephrase their answer so that you do understand.

Please use the following pages to record your interview notes. Personally, if it were me interviewing a hypnotist or hypnotherapist I would interview no less than three and I would compare their answers. Now lets talk about the financial obligation of therapy. **NEVER LET MONEY STAND IN THE WAY OF TREATMENT!** We enter the field of hypnotherapy to resolve issues, not create new ones. Often if you are honest about the financial challenges facing you, the hypnotherapist will apply a sliding fee scale. This means they reduce their fees so that you can afford their services. I wish you all the best in your journey for the Perfect Hypnotherapist.

Interview Notes

Interview Notes

Interview Notes

Interview Notes

Interview Notes

Interview Notes

Interview Notes

Interview Notes

Interview Notes

Interview Notes

Interview Notes

Interview Notes

Interview Notes

Interview Notes

Interview Notes

Interview Notes

Interview Notes

Interview Notes

Interview Notes

Interview Notes

Interview Notes

Interview Notes

Interview Notes

Interview Notes

Interview Notes

Interview Notes

Interview Notes

Interview Notes

Interview Notes

www.ingramcontent.com/pod-product-compliance
Lightning Source LLC
LaVergne TN
LVHW051131080426
835510LV00018B/2348